Not Guilty by Reason of Insanity

Victor Wirtanen

DEDICATION

I dedicate this book to NAMI who provided support and inspiration for my book.

CONTENTS

ACKNOWLEDGMENTS

Special thanks to Peggy McCarthy at NAMI who provided inspiration for my book. Also, thanks to my brother Christopher Wirtanen for his help in organizing the sections of my book. Finally, special thanks to my brother in law Ben Huumala who gave me the idea to write my story, without him the book would not have happened.

1 INTRODUCTION

"F*ck there's a body in the back, yelled the border guard" pulling out his service revolver and sticking it to my head; in my Bipolar delusional mania I calmly accepted this latest occurrence as part of a government, as well as a divine plan, educating me on who has the power in the country and the world.

The following book will cover my life and struggles with Bi-Polar. It has been an exciting eleven year Bi-Polar rollercoaster.

The following, in italics, is a writing by my mom which introduces her experience when I became affected by Bi-Polar and covers some of my early years:

I did not know much about mental illness in 2007, so I did not recognize the obvious signs of Victor going manic until he was pretty far gone. The entire spring of 2007 Victor was slipping farther and farther from reality and doing more erratic and uncharacteristic things.

We brought him to the emergency room finally and he cooperated with the professionals. He started on Zyprexa and they made him an appointment to see a psychiatrist. Not realizing the seriousness of the situation we took him back home. Hindsight tells us he

should have been admitted to the mental hospital right away but
...

Bad things had a chance to happen, an incident that brought in the police and the criminal justice system.

What a joke, maybe things have improved since then but at the time we received very little help and we were lied to and deceived by the police.

Victor had to wait in the Clark County jail for about six weeks before he was finally moved to Western State even though the judge ordered it immediately.

Criminalizing mental illness has to be the greatest crime of our society. An obviously ill person innocent to any wrong doing is dragged through the justice system and left with a criminal report.

The case got cleared up and Victor returned to sanity. Two years later he had another break. We were more in tune with the illness this time but now we hit the second great obstacle for getting help for the mentally ill. The laws are written to protect the ill person therefore he cannot be forced to accept treatment.

Again, Victor had to get so bad that he had another brush with the law and then treatment could be forced. This was in 2009.

The third break was 2011 and here we had the law on our side, Victor had to do what the doctor ordered because he was on supervised release, but we were failed by the system yet again, this time by the doctor. The doctor would not force Victor to do what he didn't want even though I pleaded with him. I told him that Victor was not Sane and that he would again get in trouble if he wasn't forced on stronger medication.

Sure enough, some more criminal acts had to be added to Victor's record before he got help.

Every time Victor slipped from sanity to insanity, his judgement left him. He quit caring about consequences and did whatever he felt like. He quit listening to his parents and quit following the teachings of his faith.

When he returned to sanity his conscience became alive and he started acting like his normal self. The line between sanity and insanity was clear to see for anyone who knew Victor. People who didn't know him could be fooled for a while.

It was a cold December when Victor was born, five weeks early. He had diaphragmatic hernia and had to have surgery right away. He recovered swiftly with no ill effects.

Our life was in a transition since Andy(Victor's father) had quit logging and tried to get into the building trades. There was a recession going on and the wages were very low. We made a decision to move to Alaska for work. We lived there for two and a half years, through three summers and two long winters. Victor has some memories of that time. He was almost three when we came back.

After some low paying jobs, Andy started working for the Washington State DOT, where he has worked ever since then, for thirty years. For nine years we also had a part time business as rental managers, which involved the whole family.

When Victor was little he wished for lots of brothers and sisters. He got his wish, though it took many years until he appreciated his younger siblings. I guess they had to grow up to be worth anything. Life was busy in a big family, there was never a dull moment. Victor was the oldest so he did have a lot of responsibility.

Through the years we made a lot of road trips, since Andy had paid leave. Trips across the US brought us as far as Michigan, as far North as Alaska and south to California. We flew to Finland and to the East Coast. Camping, boating and gardening have always been a big part of our lives.

Andy grew up in a do-it-yourself type of family and passed it on to his children. All the older children were involved in building our house, shop and sauna. Countless projects have been completed in the shop over the years.

Life seemed relatively smooth and happy until mental illness entered the picture. Victor's brother Leo had problems as a teenager already but we didn't really understand it or seek treatment for him. Also, Victor's aunt and uncle had mental problems for years.

The greatest event and one that changed our lives forever was Victor's breakdown. He started showing signs of something being wrong in the spring of 2007, but it didn't become obvious until July-August. Various horrible events happened, Victor landed in jail and then the mental hospital. These events had a profound effect on the whole family. Many of us have suffered PTSD –like symptoms. The horrible times are behind us and Victor has recovered, but it wasn't an easy nine years.

Several of Victor's siblings have suffered mental breakdowns after his, though none as severe as his. Yet, three of them have a continual struggle and have a hard time finding stability. Medicines don't seem to be effective and sleeplessness is an issue.

We have to say that much good has also come from being a part of Victor's trials and experiences. We have all gained a much better understanding of mental illness and have become more compassionate toward our fellow human beings. We find ourselves to be less judgmental and are free to speak up against the stigma that still prevails when it comes to mental illness.

It has also been wonderful to see how the family members support each other. There is so much support also from our church family and friends. Victor's experiences have touched many, many people.

As a child we took a lot of vacations. My dad works for the state of Washington in maintenance and gets over a month of vacation a year. Many times we would take short trips up into the mountains and camp out for a few days. Other times we would take longer vacations like to the redwoods in California, or to visit my cousins in Alaska. I have fond memories of traveling to Alaska, especially, and seeing the great scenery and wildlife. Later on when I got older I was able to travel to Alaska again with my brother which I detail in another chapter.

When my dad is not planning some fishing trip he can often be found in a large garden we have, as well as a green house. Also we have somewhere around one hundred fruit trees spread around the yard and in an orchard. The garden and fruit trees require a lot of upkeep which includes pulling weeds, spraying fruit trees, and also chopping and stacking wood for the fires we keep going in the house and often in the Sauna. Fortunately my mom and dad are hard workers and there are fourteen of us children so the work gets done without too much issue.

Growing up the house was unfinished much of my teenage years as my dad was building it slowly when funds came. When we had the money he would try to round up some of us kids to help him finish a section of the house, such as a bedroom. The fortunate part about building the house this way was that there was no debt associated with the house.

In addition to having a garden and fruit trees we also had some animals over the years. For many years we had goats which my dad wanted to use to pack meat for hunting and we also had a variety of dogs and chickens over the years. Trying to get the dogs to not kill the chickens was and is always a challenge but these days with shock collars it is a little easier. For a while we had ducks, but the ducks would attack the chickens so we had to get rid of them.

2 TIUAJANA

"F*ck there's a body in the back, yelled the border guard" pulling out his service revolver and sticking it to my head; in my Bipolar delusional mania I calmly accepted this latest occurrence as part of a government, as well as a divine plan, educating me on who has the power in the country and the world.

As I stepped out of the vehicle I put my hands behind my back accepting the handcuffs and told the border guards that questioned me that this was all part of my plan so that I could write a thesis focusing on economic geography and specifically focusing on the underworld and criminal element. One of the guards asked me," so part of your thesis could even involve getting arrested to learn more about the prison system? In my delusional mind I said, exactly." I was escorted into the border station and told to sit on a metal bench and wait for intake.

A few days earlier I had been enjoying the club scene in Tijuana on a manic delusional Bipolar high and had gotten coerced into accepting a job with the Coyotes, people smugglers. After I refused to spend any more money, on a woman or beer, at a club in downtown Tijuana, Mexico (TJ), a man approached me in the darkened club where I sat with a woman and a beer and asked me if I wanted to do a drive for him. In my manic state of mind I thought it sounded like a great way to make some money, so I told him I would do the job. He then told me that they would have to do some modifications to my car and that would cost some money which I would have to pay. I hopped into an SUV type vehicle with the man I had been talking to and another rough looking Hispanic and they drove me to an ATM, while some hard core rap pumped from the car stereo. I remember feeling a little scared as I considered the rough looking characters and noticed a large scar on one of their arms. I pulled out about one hundred dollars for the modifications on my car which, I learned later, included a compartment where the spare tire goes big enough to fit a human in. I was never really told what I would deliver but the men alluded to the fact that it would be people smuggling.

After I gave the men the money they told me they would be putting me up in a motel room and would take care of anything I wanted, women, drugs, prescription drugs, you name it. One of the men showed me to my room, a decent looking room kind of on a "Motel 6" scale. He then led me across the street where we picked out a meal for me, something very cheap. The problem with all of this was that I had already made reservations at a nice Tijuana motel and I was totally not going to make it to the motel I had already paid for. This was how it was when I was out of my mind though, I just kind of went with the flow and did not stress too much about other things that did not work because of new developments.

After the other man bid me goodbye, for the time being, I noticed a young man staring at me as I was making my way back to the motel room. Not sure what he wanted I wondered if he was gay because he was staring at me. Not wanting to make enemies, and thinking that he could be somebody powerful, because he was nicely dressed with a Lacoste shirt and a nice leather bag, I decided to take a walk with him. He could speak scarcely a lick of English and I could not speak much Spanish but we took a nice walk together to the ocean which was nearby. The weather was nice and warm as it always is in TJ and the sand was a beautiful white, the water a nice light blue. On the way back from our walk I had a taco from a street vendor. The meat was carved off a large chunk of meat that was just heating in the sun; it tasted decent and was very cheap, only about eighty cents.

After I got back to my motel room I decided to go explore the Starbucks on the other side of the road. I bought a Caramel Frappuccino and sat outside and listened to some music on my laptop. Next to me were a couple of young guys smoking endless cigarettes and playing cards; I imagined they were some rich kids with nothing to do but play cards and smoke, probably their dad was high up in a drug cartel. Another guy next to me was on the phone and looked very worried, I imagined he was concerned because he did not know where this rich looking white guy came from and he could have been worried for my safety. Mexico is a country of haves and have nots and everybody had their place. Starbucks was a hangout for the rich, because the prices were no different than in America.

After I finished at Starbucks I crossed the road back to my motel very carefully. In TJ there is no respect for life and the cars will speed up as you attempt to cross the road. Back in my motel room I watched a little TV and waited for nightfall. The TV channels, just like the city of TJ, were full of graphic violence. When night fell I decided to go find a taxi driver and see if he could lead me to women. I walked across the street and asked the nearest taxi driver if he could lead me to a prostitute. He told me all the prostitutes were located on La Revolution, so I told him to take me there. He drove there and while driving we chatted. He said he often used the prostitutes and that the best way to do it was to find a prostitute and use them regularly for a week or two, building a relationship. He advocated even taking them to lunch once in a while.

We arrived at La Revolution and the girls were lined up. I had my eye on a nice light skinned girl who looked almost white, but the taxi driver chose me a more traditional looking Mexican girl and one who was a little older, about my age maybe 28.

Later on the taxi driver and I headed back to my motel room and I paid him about five dollars very cheap for everything he did for me.

Back at the motel room I was still not very tired, so I decided to head to a store and buy a pack of smokes. I had run out of my traditional cigar, Al Capone Cognac Dipped Miniatures, which I learned to smoke in Europe on a trip. Seeing a man that looked to be sweeping the street next to my motel, everybody it seems has a job in Mexico even if sometimes it is just standing around with a broom, I asked him if he could escort me to the store and back, so that I could buy a pack of smokes, he said he could do that and we were on our way. The evening was warm and the streets were quiet as it was about eleven o'clock at night.

I picked up the smokes and when the man escorted me back to my motel room I hooked him up with a six pack of alcohol that I had in my room; He seemed very pleased.

The next day my car showed up with a younger Mexican at the

wheel and he told me to hop in. We were on our way to the border and presumably there was someone in the back of my vehicle. I wanted to take my luggage with me, but the people smugglers had plans of me doing multiple runs and they wanted me to leave my luggage.

I reluctantly hopped in thinking that it would look more natural if the back of my Subaru Legacy Wagon was full of luggage instead of completely empty.

The young Mexican and I started for the border, he was driving, the weather was nice and warm, the sky blue. I was supposed to make fifteen hundred dollars for each run and the Coyotes hoped to get me to do three or four runs. I myself had misgiving about making so many runs and planned on a single run and then jetting. The problem was that they had insisted that I leave my entire luggage in TJ. About ten minutes from the border the younger Mexican hopped out of the car and told me to drive the rest of the way to the border. I then turned on my soundtrack on my mp3 player and let the individual in the back listen to some Eminem. The going was slow to the border and I was feeling pensive. On the sides of the road leading to the American side were street vendors that would come to your window attempting to sell you stuff. I finally made it to the border, where I took off my sunglasses and told the border guard he was welcome to check the back of my vehicle, after he asked. He walked back to check for anything unusual, lifting the carpet covering where my spare tire usually was and noticing a body in the back promptly arrested me and escorted me to the border station.

In the border station I noticed a smooth looking fat Mexican with a gold chain and a huge wad of 100 dollar bills. He took the wad of bills and handed them to an officer and I imagined that it was money for some kind of bribe. Bribes even on the American side are not unheard of. One of the Coyotes that I was talking to in Tijuana before I attempted to cross the border told me that one of the lanes was paid for and that I should have no trouble getting through. He even gave me a cell phone to call him just before I crossed the border, so that he could inform me which lane to take.

Unfortunately bribes or no bribes I was getting no extra help and I soon found myself locked in a fairly large room with about twenty Mexicans. The talk was all about people smuggling, to begin with but then got downright dirty, as I imagined that was why most of the people in the room were there. From the room next to ours came some weird howling noises and some of the Mexicans said that was the border guards interrogating the Coyotes to try to find out more information about their operation. One of the Mexicans said the guards would hook jumper cables on to your nuts to make you talk. After everyone settled in the talk begin to get dirty and people begin to ask each other what kind of crazy things they had done. One Mexican said that he had lived on a farm and enjoyed screwing the chickens. Another said that he enjoyed eating mangos with cum. I said that I once had jacked off a cat.

3 GROWING UP

I am the oldest of fourteen children. Having big families is common in my faith, the Old Apostolic Lutheran church. My faith has always been important to me but as time goes on and I make it through good times and bad it continues to ground me and provide me with stability in an ever changing world. My faith started at birth with teachings about Jesus from my mother and father and also weekly church services on Sunday including Sunday school. In Sunday school we would go over the bible using a bible history and catechism. Sunday school lasted until I was fifteen years old and ended with confirmation. Confirmation was a recap of what we learned in Sunday school and was the time when many people take the faith for themselves, instead of just believing the same way as mom and dad. I was born in Vancouver, Washington at the Southwest Washington Medical Center. I was born with a diaphramic hernia and the doctors did not think I would make it. Miraculously I survived and early on my parents moved to Alaska for work reasons. The eighties were a slow time in Washington State and it was busier up in Alaska, in Alaska my sister was born. I have memories from early on, even when I was two years old, I remember being pulled on a sled with ice skates, piloting an airplane, which had two steering wheels, and retrieving hockey pucks for my dad when he would play hockey.

We moved down when I was three and shortly thereafter, school years begin. The neighborhood we moved into had about seven or eight families that go to our church and that meant that as I grew up I had many friends that were of the same faith. In a way we were almost our own little community. After school, almost every day, I would go to a friend's house or invite a friend over. We would often do outside activities such as football, soccer, skateboarding, or riding our bikes. Then likely as not a friend would stay for dinner or I would eat dinner at a friend's house. These friends that I grew up with are still friends today and are becoming pillars in the congregation, in other words all of us are becoming important parts of the Old Apostolic Lutheran Faith.

I had some trouble in school early on because my family, excluding my dad, was bilingual. My mother's family immigrated from Finland, so Finnish is all that I heard at home from my mom. Being bilingual I sometime had trouble pronouncing words the American way and in class I would sometime use Finnish words. At first they put me in a special education class, but I hated it and soon grew out of it.

My life growing up was not extremely typical for a number of reasons, as I alluded to when I mentioned I grew up in a tight knit religious community. My mom was constantly having babies which meant the house was getting filled and there was more and more action. In our faith we believe that a woman should have as many children as God gives them, I believe this ties in with the commandment to be fruitful and replenish the earth. We also grew up with no television or radio. My dad did have a radio if there was an earthshaking event like a war, but other than that we had to make up our own entertainment. I spent a lot of time at the neighbors, playing football, skateboarding, riding bicycles, etc.

The reason we have no television is because with the faith I belong to we hold it to be sin. There is just nothing edifying on television, and if there is, it is hidden under a mountain of loose moral behavior. We follow the doctrine of Christ and all the apostles which, of course, includes everything in the bible. Some would call our faith very strict, but it is the faith I grew up in and the one that I believe will bring me to heaven. You the reader might wonder why I bring my faith into the book and explain it, but it is important for a number of reasons. First of all my faith is what keeps me grounded and helps keep me off the streets. Second of all, when I am manic the teachings of my faith go completely out the window, which is an important lesson.

As you have read previously, when I was manic and not properly medicated, I fornicated, drank beer, did drugs, frequented strip clubs, committed crimes, and did all manner of ungodly activity and activity that goes directly against my strong moral upbringing and the teachings in my faith. In addition, I did all of these activities without feeling the least bit of guilt. In fact, I can remember when I lost my conscience and then later regained it when I was properly medicated.

Normally when and if I commit something that is against the teachings of God, such as looking at pornography, Jesus says, "if you look upon a woman to lust after her, you have already committed adulatory in your heart." It will come on my conscious and I will go ask forgiveness for it from a pastor in our faith or another one of my Christian brothers. When my medication was not correct I simply did not feel bad about a thing. I also had extreme delusions of grandeur; at one point of my mania I thought that I was Jesus Christ. At another point in time I thought that I was talking directly with God. As I was so delusional, I believed that none of the standard teachings applied to me and I could do as I pleased. I really enjoyed this carefree life of going to strip clubs, chilling out in the lawn chair and drinking Hawaiian Longboard Lager, and in general doing as I pleased. However, as soon as I got to Western State and was properly medicated I became sane from insane and returned to the battle against sin and the fight to retain strong morals. This does not mean that it is easy to walk forward in my life and not fall into sin. In fact, some of the habits that I picked up while crazy die hard and I must often go and confess to the pastor where I have fallen into sin. However, I no longer live openly in sin and I battle against sin daily. Finally, I believe that a willful life of sin could take me to Hell and I would rather avoid that place, I've already been to the Clark County Jail that was bad enough.

So what keeps me living a moral life, and off the streets, instead of living the life I lived while insane? As I mentioned earlier, going to hell is a strong motivator, but for me that alone is not enough. A big part of what keeps me living clean is that I live with my parents and I abide by the rules of the house. Also, I have hundreds if not thousands of church friends that I could no longer look straight in the eyes the next time I saw them; we are like one big family in the Old Apostolic Lutheran Church and when one of the members goes astray, all of the members know and feel it. As it says in the bible, being one body of Christ. Just an example of how tight knit we are, when I needed letters of reference for an application for a Presidential Pardon I could easily get them with no questions asked. While there was no way for any of the people who wrote me references to know exactly what I did on my spare time, they trusted me completely and attested to my sound moral character. I appreciate their trust and would not want to do anything to break that trust.

Now that you understand a little more about my upbringing and faith I will move on to the rest of my teenage years and my life before having my first breakdown. When I was sixteen I got my first job, at Fred Meyer, pushing carts, cleaning, and helping people out of the store with their groceries. This was a good for some gas money and spending money in general. I was pretty busy up until my breakdown and one summer I even worked two jobs one summer, one at Fred Meyer and the other at a local concrete foundation company. I would get about four or five hours of sleep a night and about an hour nap, until the weekend.

What would I do with my free time? Well, I was pretty busy so I did not have much free time but I remember spending some summer's wakeboarding in the evening with my friend Jarret, who had a boat, and other friends, going rollerblading in Portland or Vancouver on the waterfronts and just hanging out with friends in the evenings, drinking mountain dew and visiting. On Sundays my friends and I would spend a few hours in church and then spend the rest of our day eating at a barbecue joint, and driving around in the hills glassing for elk and deer. Today, I spend less time in the hills on Sunday and more time at a Christian's house visiting about a question from the bible.

The bible we use where we find questions is the standard King James Version and each Sunday the pastor takes a text from the bible and it is read. He then preaches alongside that passage from the bible with nothing planned out in advance. We, the congregation, believe that he is enlightened by God's Holy Spirit and that his preaching is the word of God.

Where did the Old Apostolic Lutheran faith come from you may wonder. Old Apostolic's believe upon all of the teachings of Jesus Christ and his Apostles; therefore our faith came directly from Christ. There are a few notable figures in our faith since Jesus, a couple of them being Martin Luther and Lars Levi Laestadius. Most people know who Martin Luther was, but fewer people have heard of Lars Levi Laestadius. Laestadius, a Swedish minister, found our faith and began to spread it throughout Swedish Lapland. This faith which he spread then spread to America through immigrants and is the same faith that I practice today.

After a few years at Fred Meyer, I quit that and started working only with concrete work until noon every day; in the afternoon I would go to Clark College. At first I was still in high school and I was able to do the running start program through the welding program. I had become an expert welder in high school and had taken every class they offered. Because of that I was able to take welding classes at Clark College, specifically a type of welding called TIG welding. After a while though, I tired of welding, and began taking general classes for a business degree.

4 MOTORCYCLE TRIP

I had just quit working for Dean's Concrete and had been working for Cascade Vinal Deck for three or four months when my buddy Glen and I decided to take our motorcycles to Spearfish South Dakota to go to church meetings. Both of us had bought road bikes about a year back and we were yearning to test them out on a longer road trip. Glen had a Honda Shadow 1100 and I had a GS 450 L Suzuki. My bike was a little small for a longer road trip but it was pretty snappy and could keep up with Glen's bike without too much trouble.

Working for the deck and fence company was fun as a friend and I were working together. We would quickly install wood decks and vinal coverings for wood posts. The boss of the firm was not too excited when I told him that a friend and I had road trip planned to Spearfish, but I had let him know right when I started that I had a trip planned, so he was okay with it.

It was sunny out and about mid-June as Glen and I filled up the saddlebags on our motorcycles and threw on our back packs, preparing to embark on our journey. Glen took off in the lead and I followed behind. Just down the road we got pulled over for going a little over the speed limit and Glen got a ticket. I got let off the hook because the cop radared Glen and not me. What a way to start a trip but at least it was not me that got the ticket. Then a few more hours into our trip Glen ran out of gas. His motorcycle would not travel as far as mine between tanks and early on in our trip he had not found that out yet. I traveled the few additional miles to the gas station and bought a spare tank for gas and brought Glen the gas, unfortunately some of the gas drained out on my clothes in my backpack and my clothes stunk like gas until they got a chance to air out.

One instant that sticks in my mind is going over a bridge into the tri-cities and the wind was blowing very hard. The wind was really blowing around my motorcycle and I had to really lean so that it would not blow me over. In the evening we arrived in Davenport, Washington, with bug splattered windshields, and spent the night at a local preachers house who is a friend of the family.

The weather was cool in the morning and we ate breakfast and got ready to continue are journey. We continued are routine, filling up for gas every one hundred miles or so as we cruised through the mountain passes of Idaho and Montana. We began to get very comfortable riding our motorcycles and we would kick back with our feet on the gas tank, cruising at around eighty miles an hour. About ten hours into our trip we arrived at our second stop, the Shoosters. The Shoosters were a family that went to our church and who I knew from prior visits to their house when traveling through Billings, Montana. I distinctly remember the woman of the house commenting, those are nice machines, when we pulled up to their house for the night. The motorcycles did look nice, but I was suffering with a chain that constantly would stretch out at the high speeds and Glen was suffering with some type of engine problems which would cause the motorcycle to sputter, often his bike would get too much fuel. None the less, the problems were fairly minor and we would continue on our journey to Spearfish the next day.

In Spearfish, we rented a motel room with some other friends that were going to meetings as well and I took my bike to the motorcycle shop to get a new chain put on. Meetings were nice and we enjoyed the weekend listening to the word of God, going to gatherings to discuss the word of God, spending time at the park watching or playing volleyball, going to get togethers in the evenings and meeting new friends and we even gave a few girls motorcycle rides up Spearfish Canyon.

After meetings Glen and I heard that some friends were meeting in Sheridan, Wyoming where we could play some more volleyball and go spelunking. Volleyball was great as it was nice and sunny and we played on sand volleyball courts. One day we all decided to go and explore a nearby cave which had a waterfall deep inside it. We grabbed headlamps and flashlights and hiked down into the cave. We had to go down quite a ways and at one point we climbed through a hole to a passageway below. At the point where we crawled through I put a small pile of rocks as a reminder of where we needed to stop and climb up to get back out. The pile of rocks turned out to be a blessing, because it is likely we would have walked right by the opening in the roof, had I not left the pile of rocks. Apparently the waterfall deep inside the cave was neat, but I decided not to go see it because you had to take your shoes off and wade a while to get to it.

A few days later we left Sheridan and drove to Kalispell, Montana where we had friends and where we would spend the weekend. In Kalispell I met a nice Christian girl, for the first time and we later got to know each other a little better. After Kalispell we finished our trip with our faltering bikes. My motorcycles clutch cable broke and Glen's bike was still having engine troubles. After Kalispell to home I shifted my motorcycle without a clutch and tried to avoid as many traffic lights as possible as it was difficult to get going without a clutch.

Even with the minor motorcycle troubles the trip was epic and I am reminded of that trip often when I drive my motorcycle today. The Suzuki I had has since been replaced by a bigger Suzuki Intruder 800 and I look forward to summer, when I can take my motorcycle for a ride again.

5 FINLAND

In the winters while I was going to college I would spend time with my grandparents in Finland. In Finland I met many friends and I just blended in, largely because I am fluent in the Finnish language. On one occasion I met a Canadian who was visiting Finland and who was fluent in Finnish, named Marcus. Marcus and I hit it off and we decided to go for a day trip to Estonia. The ferry travels from Helsinki, Finland to Tallinn, Estonia in a matter of hours. Marcus and I got dropped off at the ferry terminal early in the morning and for around 15 dollars we were able to buy tickets to go to Estonia. Traveling on the ferry was neat as you could go on the upper deck and see the cold Baltic Sea below. There were also a lot of slot machines on the ferry but as we did not gamble, we had no use for the machines.

It was still morning when we arrived in Tallinn and we had around eight hours to explore the town. We had a small map we had gotten from somewhere, showing us around the tourist district and we used this map to explore many old churches on old cobblestone streets. Unfortunately, at some point we got out of the area that the map covered and we entered into the poorer area of Tallinn. Fortunately for us, we were not ready to go back yet, so we found a small pizza place and bought personal pizzas and pop for only a few dollars. The waitresses were cute so we left them a big tip, which probably was not the usual custom for Estonia. Also, the waitresses showed us how to get back to the tourist area.

After a while of walking it was getting later and we still were not sure how to get back to the docks. I tried asking some local guys that I saw in the street and at a restaurant and they all turned me down saying they did not speak English. I then asked only cute girls and they were more than happy to direct me to the harbor. This was fine with me because I would rather talk with cute girls anyway.

When we got to the harbor the passengers had already boarded the ferry and the people at the ferry terminal claimed we would have to take the next ferry. Not content with waiting for the next ferry when I could see our ferry below loading cars I decided to go to the station agent where they were loading the cars and question him. At first he told us that it was too late that we would not be able to board, but at the last minute one of the guards changed their mind and stamped our passports. We then ran on to the loading dock where they loaded the cars and into the hold. The man in charge of the hold then gave us a tour of the hold and led us upstairs to the passenger deck. It was all very exciting times.

Back upstairs on the Ferry I crashed out on the floor and one Finnish girl noticed me and exclaimed that it looked like I had been drinking because I was completely burnt out. I then got up to show her I was doing okay and she then asked if I would buy her a drink, she was probably underage. I told her I would do no such thing and that it was against my religion to drink. We then talked for a while and she could not believe I was American because I spoke such good Finnish. I then showed her my passport and she believed me after that. After a while we quit talking and she got bored of me because I would not buy her a drink. She then turned her attention to a man next to her who had a case of Lappish Gold Beer and they begin making out and drinking together. This is the type of party life that happens on the ferries, but sometimes you have to take them to get from point A to point B.

Back in Finland I jumped in with some friends and we went to Christmas meetings in Gallivare, Sweden. Swedish Lapland is the home of the elders in our church and every year there are meetings held in Sweden which many Old Apostolic Christian's attend. When we got to Sweden my friends dropped me off at the church, so I could meet up with some Swedish friends of mine whose house I would be staying at. I enjoy making friends with foreigners and when they come out to the U.S. on vacation I will often show them around. Now they would be the ones showing me around.

The church in Gallivare was very small and since they have built a bigger one. We would listen to sermons from the elders crammed on small wooden benches. Then we would line up to eat and would wait for over an hour to eat. The food was very good, often reindeer meat. Usually when there was not church we would cram into small houses and discuss the word of God. In the evenings after church would get out I would go to some cabins on the ski hill where the Finns were staying and visit with them. The sermons were all translated from Swedish to Finnish, so I would have no trouble understanding the sermons without a headset. Americans who did not know Finnish or Swedish received English translation into headsets which they would wear.

After Christmas meetings were over I hopped in with some Swedes and Americans in a van and we headed to Norway for New Year's meetings. My Finnish friends had traveled back to Finland. In Norway we attended a few days of church and I was also able to spend some time with my dad's sisters family who lived in Breivik, Norway. My dad's sister and her husband live on a rocky knoll overlooking the choppy waters of a fjord. All around are rocky mountains and water, it is some of the most scenic area in the world. I still remember attending a New Year's Eve gathering in Norway and listening to the preacher talk to us young kids as fireworks went off outside, it was very peaceful.

After the meetings were over and I had visited my aunt and uncle for a while, I took a train from Narvik, Norway to Stockholm, Sweden. On this train I met some Christian friends and I visited with one of them for many hours, in fact, we visited all night about what I know not and in the morning the Swede I was with called his dad and they tried to figure out the best way I could get from Sweden back to Finland. It was decided I should fly from Stockholm to Finland as I was pressed for time and I got off the train and hiked to the airport which was a few mile hike. I then got on a computer which was in the airport and bought a one way ticket to Helsinki. After a short flight I was back in Helsinki and ready for my trip back to the USA.

Over the years I have been to Europe five times and I feel blessed to have been able to go so many times. While I have had a lot of pain and suffering in my life I certainly have had a lot of high points. My most recent trip was to Europe for over two months and this was a much needed vacation after being on probation for over three years.

6 ELK HUNTING

While I have not been hunting in years, I still have fond memories of going elk hunting with my dad in the early fall of one summer in my late teens. These days my dad hunts elk and deer with a rifle and because I have a felony on my record I am not allowed to use firearms. Back then my dad and I bow hunted and we would spend time up near Mount Saint Helens watching Elk and trying to get close enough to them to down one.

It was early September and my dad and I packed up our gear to go hunting. We had been practicing shooting our bows at paper plates in the back yard and both of us could shoot accurately enough to hit a paper plate regularly at about thirty yards, around fifty to sixty feet. In addition to shooting my bow in the back yard I remember a trip my friends and I took to an inside shooting range with moving targets, called Broken Arrow. All of the practice honed my skills and I felt ready to take down an elk if we found one when we went hunting.

If we did down an elk we had goats that would help us pack the meat out. A few years prior to our going hunting my dad had bought three goats and had trained them to pack meat. Using goats was unusual but it was something my dad wanted to try. We loaded up the goats into the back of my dad's truck as well as our gear on a Monday morning and traveled to Mount Saint Helens. We parked our truck and started hiking up the narrow dirt trail with the goats. About five miles later after climbing up the winding trail we found a place to camp on the side of a hillside where we could see a valley below where there proved to be elk. Some of the time we would spend glassing for the elk, there was a couple of big bulls, six pointers or so, with a lot of cows. Then we would slowly and quietly as possible travel down to where the elk were and try to get close enough for a shot. The hunting unit we were in was three points minimum, which means we could not shoot any cows or any elk that had less than three points. The three point minimum rule was so the bulls had a chance to grow up before they got shot. We trailed the herd multiple times and got very close to it but never close enough for a shot. When we got closer the herd would smell us and run away and we would hike for miles trailing the herd. During the entire process I got in very good shape because we would hike all day up and down hills. At the end of the week we wrapped up our elk hunting and headed for home. I had seen a lot of new territory including a few lakes we hiked to and of course lots of big elk. Hunting was a very fun relaxing time and a great way to get in shape. When we got back home I remember how easy it was running up our hill which I did on one occasion to test how good of shape I was in. It is amazing how much weight you can lose in four or five days and also how much your physical ability can improve.

Someday I would like to go bow hunting again but as it is with any fun experience it is enjoyable to think of when you might get the chance to do it again.

7 ALASKA

It was summer of 2005 and I was packing panels in Tri-Cities Washington. In other words, I was doing concrete construction work in the hot sun and blowing dirt and sand in Eastern Washington. Panels are large two foot by eight foot sheets of one inch plywood that are coated in diesel and used to form up the walls of house foundations. The crew I was working with was working out of town. We were based out of the Vancouver, Washington area but a builder we worked for wanted some work done in Tri-Cities and my boss decided to take the job because the price was right. Doing work in Tri-Cities was a change of pace from are usual work as it was hot and dry. In the Vancouver area it is often wet and muddy and doing foundation work can become a drag.

While I was working one day in the hot sun I had a thought, it sure would be nice to take a trip to Alaska. I had cousins that live in Alaska and I had been up their a few times previously. During the first few years of my life we lived there, and then our entire family took a road trip up to Alaska when I was in the seventh grade. I really enjoyed the road trip with my parents and I decided it would be nice to do the road trip again either alone or with a friend.

After we were finished working in Tri-Cities I sat down and had a talk with my boss Dean and told him about my thoughts of going to Alaska. Dean thought it was a great idea and said that if he was my age he would do the same thing. After talking with Dean a little, he said that he could not guarantee a job for me when I came back down, but since I was planning on taking classes at Clark College anyway, and also had a decent amount saved up, I was not too worried about whether I would have a job when I came back.

After talking the trip over with my mom and dad we decided that it would be good if my younger brother Esa would make the trip up to Alaska with me and then he would fly down not staying for quite as long as I planned to stay. I planned to stay for over a month and fish part of the time and work part of the time. I had heard that jobs were plentiful in Alaska in the summer and that the pay was good.

On July 24th we took off for Alaska and drove over twenty hours straight to Chetwin, Canada where my friend Tyrol was managing a crew of tree planters. He had went to school for a few years as a forestry technician and was earning some money in the summer. Tyrol lived in a small cabin on the corner of a large ranch. Dead tired my brother and I pulled into the yard and Tyrol was still at work. He had left the cabin door open though, so we threw are sleeping bags on the floor and went to sleep until he came home. Tyrol had a fairly interesting job where getting out to where the trees needed planted required a helicopter.

When evening came Tyrol came home and we had a nice visit before we went to sleep again and woke up the next morning ready for the next leg of our journey. You might wonder how I had a friend in Northern Canada, but Tyrol is a member of our church and I had gone to confirmation with him and had known him for years.

Back on the road we stopped for gas at small Indian villages next to large lakes and rivers and enjoyed the scenery as we drove up through the Yukon. When we got tired we would stop and pitch a tent fairly close to the road, but nonetheless in the middle of the wilderness. I remember one morning we stopped in Whitehorse a fairly large northern Canadian town and stocked up on supplies in a grocery store. We then had breakfast at the top of a windswept knoll and continued on our way.

About thirty six hours later, not counting our rest stops to camp we crossed into Alaska from Canada. We had no trouble at the borders, to speak of, other than the Canadians did a routine search when we entered into Canada. Before we went to sleep for the night on US territory again, I couldn't help but reflect on all of the neat scenery we had just passed through. One nice spot was a hot springs we checked out where some travelers have seen bear in the past.

Forty Four hours later we arrived at my Aunt and Uncles and boy were they surprised to see us. I had told my cousin Kevin that we were going to be coming to Alaska but apparently he had forgotten to tell his mom. We enjoyed a good dinner that evening with my Aunt and Uncle Karl and Claire and then they showed us to the place Esa and I would be staying. We started out sleeping in the basement and then later on when Esa went home I moved to the Upstairs of Carl's shop.

My time in Alaska was either spent fishing or working. While Esa was with me I did not work at all. We both bought fishing licenses and would go to Jim creek and usually limit out within the first few hours. Fishing was easy; you just put the eggs in an egg loop, threw the line out, and jerked a little when you felt a fish nibble. Usually we would catch a fish every cast. We did our fishing either from the bank or from a canoe.

One morning that sticks in my mind was after Esa was gone. I had stayed up all night reading paperback novels and then about six o'clock, took off in my cousins Blazer with a canoe tied on top headed for Jim Creek. After paddling across a lake and pulling the canoe across a gravel bar which separated Jim Creek from Jim Lake, I got into Jim Creek and threw out a line. I quickly reeled in two fishes and then a third. On my third fish the hook got caught way back in its mouth. It was a large male buck salmon and had a large hooked mouth. I grabbed my Leatherman and tried to fish the hook out but the fish snapped at my fingers and I dropped my Leatherman in the water. The water was pretty shallow so I decided to step in and try to retrieve it which proved to be a mistake. The bottom of the creek was very muddy and I sank in. Fortunately I was able to get back into the canoe, but my Leatherman was gone for good. All in all though, a good adventure and a good example of the fun times I had fishing.

Before Esa left we had over two coolers full of frozen fish and we decided to make smoked salmon. Mixing a brine of one half brown sugar, and one half salt, we let the fishes soak overnight and then put them in a large commercial smoker which a friend of ours had, another friend from church. After the fishes were smoked I ended up with half a cooler full of smoked salmon which I would bring back down with me after I left Alaska.

Since I did hope to make a little money while I was up in Alaska, and since life is not all about fishing, I was able to land a couple of short one week stints helping out friends from church. The first opportunity for work was for a man a few years older than me who was building a shop. He needed help with the sheetrock and the vapor barrier. Most people know what sheetrock is, which covers the walls and which the paint goes on. However, many people may not have heard of vapor barrier as it is only required in colder climates. The vapor barrier is plastic sheeting which goes on the wall and protects the insulation and sheetrock from moisture caused by the extreme difference in temperatures between the outside air and the inside air. Without a vapor barrier cold outside air would condensate and water would soak into the insulation and sheetrock. This would cause the walls to rot and ruin them. I worked for this young man on his shop for about a week and then he was able to get one of his brothers to help him finish the job.

My next job I landed was carrying bricks and mud for masons working on the house of a local builder. He wanted large brick pillars and a decorative archway for his new house. Since it was hard to find masons in Alaska that wanted to tackle such a small job, he flew up a couple of masons from Washington State and volunteered to take them fishing in addition to paying them wages. My cousin Kevin and I worked hard carrying hod as it's called, and after a week or so the job was complete. I was offered a job working for the builder helping him finish odds and ends on various jobs, but I had school to go to back home. Besides that, the snow was starting to come in on the tops of the mountain peaks that surround the Matanuska Valley where I was staying and I knew that if I wanted to get back home with no trouble, the time was now.

On or about September 1st I said my goodbyes, took my half a cooler full of smoked salmon, and hit the road. For the way back I decided to take a more scenic road called the Stewart Cassiar, on the way up I took the Alcan. The Steward Cassiar would go directly through a small town called Vanderhoof where we had fifty or so Christians that go to my church. If I traveled quick enough I would make it to Missionary meetings we were having in Vanderhoof, and then I could continue on and hit meetings in another locality called Summerland, and then Davenport WA. and finally I would make a small detour to visit friends in Kalispell, Montana and then make it back home for school to start on about the twentieth of September.

I traveled for thirty three hours with three hours of sleep through some of the most beautiful country on earth. The Stewart Cassiar is a winding road surrounded by small lakes, marshes, and bogs. Trees are everywhere, but none of them are too big. The area is also filled with wildlife, birds, bears, moose, etc.

Thirty three hours later I showed up at my forester friend's mom and dad's house in the morning and asked if they had a place I could crash out at. My relationship with this family, and many of the families in Vanderhoof is very close as I have traveled up there many times for church meeting as I mentioned in another spot, basically we are one big family.

On the way down I had feasted on Smoked Salmon and crackers, but fortunately I still had some to give to my friends in Vanderhoof. In fact, for thirty three hours I had eaten nothing except Smoked Salmon and Crackers. As I write this I am missing the smoked salmon, I may have to buy some soon.

Meetings in Vanderhoof were nice and the fellowship with friends was a big part of it. After the weekend I headed for Summerland looking forward to visiting with more friends. In Summerland, the Christians are from Finland, so they speak Finnish like me. I really enjoy speaking Finnish from time to time as it reminds me of my trips to Finland. Finnish is all I hear at home from my mother, so this helps ensure that I remain fluent. Summerland was eventful as they had me read Laestadius. Before each sermon from a preacher a sermon from a Laesadius Postilla is read. The Laestadius postillas are sermons that were recorded, as was required because Laestadius was a Lutheran Minister in the Swedish State Church. We consider Laestadius to be the first and best preacher in the time we practice our faith and therefore we read his sermons during church services. Anyway, I was the only visitor to the Summerland meetings that time, so they decided to have me read the Laestadius in the morning and in the evening. This came as a shock to me as I am not used to doing something like this, but after I got going with the reading it was not that big of a deal.

After Summerland meetings were over I enjoyed the meetings in Davenport and then took off for Kalispell. I had many friends in Kalispell and also a girl that I was interested in, which was kind of an ulterior motive. Finally, I took off for home and started classes at Clark College with the hope of getting a Business Degree later on.

I still keep up with my connections in Canada and Alaska and I recently traveled to both places for church meetings. This time in Alaska, my cousin, who I carried hod with previously, has a nice house and a wife and many kids. I enjoyed staying at his house for the last few years. Last year I went fishing with him and another cousin of mine, and this year I went to church meetings. A few months ago, I drove up to Canada with a few friends and stayed at the same house I had stayed at previously, my forester friend's mom and dad's house. In some ways I have come a full circle, but hopefully I have grown wiser in the process.

8 SNOWBOARDING

Snowboarding has always been a big part of my life. Just the other day I took off to Mount Hood Meadows with my brother Timo, as we had both purchased season passes for night skiing. I have been snowboarding for the past eighteen years and I still enjoy going up to the mountain, even though it is not as exciting as when I was in my early twenties.

When we got up to the mountain we took off up the express lift and headed up to North Canyon. After a few runs down North Canyon cruising at top speed carving in the somewhat sloppy snow we headed over to South Canyon where the half pipe and the terrain park was. Standing on my snowboard at the top of the terrain park I could not help but reflect what it was like when I was in my early twenties. Back then I enjoyed taking the biggest jumps and sailing through the air. Sometimes I cleared twenty to thirty feet of jump and was up in the air fifteen or so feet above the jump. I would then land on the downhill slope on the other side of the jump and would sometime yell out in exhilaration as I landed. The feeling of sailing through the air was one of the best feelings in the world. Now that I am older I have more fear and I imagine what would happen if I failed to land on my board on a jump. Landing on your board is important as you are so high in the air that a failure to do so could lead to serious injury. These days I just dream about what it was like to take the big air and snowboarding does not have quite the thrill it had back in the day.

In addition to the jumps were rails, fun boxes, and the rainbow rail. I really enjoyed the easier rails and especially the rainbow rail. The rainbow rail is a rail that arches from the ground in a rainbow shape and one which you can ride over on your snowboard. The nice thing about the rainbow rail is that if you fall off you generally don't land on the rail but just land in the snow unhurt. In addition to the terrain park at Mount Hood Meadows I enjoyed a few times snowboarding at Timberline Lodge and at Ski Bowl, with friends. One spring a friend and I went to Timberline and we really enjoyed taking the somewhat smaller jumps then Meadows and riding across the rails. Also when you take the top lift at Timberline you are nearly at the top of Mount Hood and the view is impressive.

A few jumps that stick in my head are at Meadows when I hit a jump extremely fast and cleared the entire jump. I remember thinking that I was really going to be hurt badly, but then I landed the jump on the flat on the other side of the jump and hit extremely hard, but survived. After that jump a girl I was with said that I didn't need to be taking such big jumps as we had just met and she did not want to lose me so soon. Another jump that sticks in my mind was one I didn't clear completely and landed so that my snowboard stuck in the top of the jump and my face hit the top of the jump. Fortunately I was not hurt bad. Finally, another jump I took I landed on my board but then did a couple of back rolls and landed back on my board. The people on the ski lift were happy with my performance which led them to cheer and then I cheered as well, all in all fun times on the mountain.

9 WSU

It was May of 2007 and I was set to graduate with a Bachelor in
Business Administration Finance with an Accounting Minor honors
included, I was 23 years old. My five years at Washington State
University Vancouver and Clark College were blessed years.
I remember jogging to my first class at WSU one morning about
ten o'clock and seeing some friends of mine doing masonry work
on the school and thinking that I was very lucky that I was able to
start classes at around ten thirty and study exactly what I enjoyed,
Finance instead of having to work doing a job I did not enjoy. I
showed up in my class and sat back with my baseball cap pulled
low and prepared to enjoy the upcoming lecture on market
theory and derivatives. The teacher John was very excited about
the subject matter and most of us enjoyed his lectures. The
learning came easy and John even mentioned one day that I really
seemed to grasp the subject matter.

Not content with just leaving the subject matter in the classroom,
I began to build up a portfolio of hand-picked stocks based on the
fundamentals of each company. If I was not attending class I could
be found working in the computer lab where I would help out
students with computing tasks. When I was not helping them I
would be researching stocks or reading the Wall Street Journal. If I

was not working, studying, or attending class I would go to the small gym and work out or go on a jog with a friend. A friend and I would jog around five miles every so often and my friend tried to keep upping the amount that we ran. I told him that I was happy with five miles every so often as I did not need to get too carried away and get burned out.

WSU Vancouver is a series of red brick buildings with a fountain in the middle of the buildings. Sidewalks extend in either direction and from one direction you can see Mount Saint Helens and the other direction you could see Mount Hood. All in all, the scene was peaceful, the scenery was beautiful, the subject matter was enjoyable, and the girls were pretty. My time at WSU was some of the best times of my life for sure.

 I was studying what I was good at, Finance, so while I had to work hard, the results were excellent. I worked part-time while I went to school, mostly in construction, but about a year and a half in the WSU computer lab assisting students, so that gave me enough money to travel and pay for expenses. Before I graduated I had made two trips to Europe, for church meetings, and numerous other cross country trips to go to church meetings and meet friends. I also spent a few weeks in Alaska visiting cousins and snowmobiling. Life seemed full of opportunities even looking at what I had within the school system. My full tuition was paid for by financial aid and I made eleven dollars an hour working in the computer labs on work study. When I was not helping a student with a computer related problem, I was reading the Wall Street Journal, or investing. By the time I graduated, and shortly before my breakdown, I had around twelve thousand dollars, mostly in the stock market, and zero debt.

While I was in the computer lab one day my friend Matt came up to me and said Dr. Umesh, a marketing professor at WSU had been trying to get some individuals to enter the Gonzaga Business Plan Competition at Gonzaga University. I was kind of busy, so I was not too excited about the idea but we decided to give it a try anyway. My cousin Reuben, who was always coming up with new inventions agreed to let Matt and I use his idea for a movable stackable safety barrier for roofing jobs. Reuben called it the Hardi-Cone and paid to have a couple of prototypes built. Matt and I worked on a business plan for the products including five years of financials. The competition was to have a grand prize of $7,500 dollars and Matt and I would split the profit if we won. Reuben would reap the benefits of our work on the plans and could use them to attract investors in his product.

A month or so later Matt and I had finished the business plan and Reuben had given us a prototype of his cone to take to the competition. The cone we were to take with us was very heavy but that was how Reuben wanted it. We told him he could cut the cone weight in half and use more cones, thereby doubling sales; he wanted nothing to do with that idea because he wanted his cone to be truly hardy.

Matt and I both grabbed our suits; I had bought a $350 dollar pin-stripe suit for the occasion, and hopped into my Volkswagen Jetta taking off for Spokane. Matt drove part of the way there and on the way a semi-truck cut us off and we nearly got in a wreck. We showed up in Spokane about four in the morning and rented a motel room for a few hours until the competition, which started around eight. I was all full of energy and only slept for about three hours, before I jogged to McDonalds and bought breakfast.

Back at the motel room we dressed up and went to Gonzaga for the competition. The competition was stiff and the judges were real business people, angel funders and venture capitalists. Both of us went through our parts and neither of us had any idea how we did. Later on we found out that we won the first prize $7,500 dollars. I flew to Spokane to accept the prize and at the same time I was getting calls to interview with a few different investment firms.

I had quite a bit going on, what with graduating, winning the business plan completion, and interviewing with a couple investment firms. Juggling all the tasks came easy, as did explaining why I was the right candidate for the firms. One of the firms had a multi stage interview process and the outside recruiter kept exclaiming how I had all the right answers. Interviewing was fun and exciting and I imagined working at a big name firm and driving a Maserati. I was a natural at Finance and my Finance teachers had high hopes of seeing me at a big ticket firm like Goldman Sachs.

After I graduated I had applied for a number of Finance jobs and I had two interviews, one with a company called Bohemian Companies and another one with Fisher Investments. During these interviews and also during the Gonzaga Business Plan Competition I was manic but not delusional. The mania probably helped me in the interview process and winning the Gonzaga Business Plan Competition because I was very excited and my mind was very sharp and fast.

With Bohemian companies I would not have gotten the interview had it not been for a classmate that told me she was interviewing for a position with Bohemian and the Chief Investment Officer had told her he was interested in interviewing me.

I had answered a questioner that Bohemian had put out about

investing and he had really liked my answers. He had asked questions like: according to efficient market theory the market is fairly priced, what makes you think you can do better than the market. I had answered, the market may be fairly priced but it is skilled individuals and their analysis which makes the markets efficient and ensures that you are getting a fair price when buying a stock, therefore a skilled analyst can be part of the process that makes the market efficient and thereby they can earn their pay. These types of answers had really grabbed the CIO and he was interested in talking to me. In fact, he had sent me an email but it had gone to my junk mail folder and unfortunately I had never seen it.

By the time I replied to the CIO he had already interviewed a number of candidates and the investors of this private wealth fund had flow from Colorado to talk to them. The CIO told me in an email that my chances of getting hired were slim but that he would like me to come in and talk to him anyway. I went in for the interview wearing my pinstripe suit and we talked about investing for a while. He then gave me an investing task to do over the weekend and I left the office and started on the task right of way.

The task had to do with looking at three investment options that were available and choosing which one would be the closest fit to the investment firm's objectives of stability and long-term price appreciation. I read through sixty pages of annual reports and finally came up with what I felt was the best investment for this firm based on their objectives. I then compiled my analysis into a one page report and sent it to him. In my reading through the annual reports I was able to find the exact same investment objective for one of the companies being studied, as the objective for his firm. I made sure to let him know in my analysis that I had found the same objective for one of the firms studied as his firm. I am sure I nailed it but he sent me an email a while later that said, "You are very bright but we will not be needing your services." Because I showed up so late in the interview process, I am sure it made it impossible to higher me.

At the same time as I was interviewing with Bohemian, I was talking with a recruiter who was contracting with Fisher Investments to higher an investment representative to super rich clients. The recruiter and I quickly built a rapport as I was excited about Fisher and had all of the answers she was looking for. I was talking fast and smooth as the mania was taking hold. I remember being very happy as I thought that I would soon be making six figures and driving a Mercedes.

After being vetted by the outside recruiter I had a phone interview with a representative from Fisher Investments. He seemed very impressed by me and was particularly impressed when he heard I enjoyed going on a ten mile bike ride with half of it up steep hills. We set up a time for me to come into the office and talk about the position in person. I went in the next day and after announcing my name at the intercom at the door it opened up and I entered in. Casey met me and we exchanged greetings and went to a room off to the side of the work area where the representatives fielded calls to clients with at least half a million in their account. While the representatives fielded the calls they threw around a beach ball to keep up the energy.

Casey asked me a few questions and then I asked if I could tour the facility. He said sure and we walked around while he explained what was going on. During Casey's questioning I remember him being impressed that I had read Ken Fishers book on investing called "The Only Three Questions that count." After reading Ken's book I completely agreed with his investment style and I was looking forward to working for his firm. However, just as I was leaving I was hit with an epiphany, these individuals talking on the phone and playing with the beach ball were stuck in their roles and although they were making great money they were not completely free. I then decided that I was destined for greater things and while I did not plan to turn down a job offer, being manic and becoming absentminded, I lost my phone and was not able to get back to Fisher if they tried to call me.

10 FIRST BREAKDOWN

The weekend, after the Fisher interview, I was walking through the woods, when I began to hear voices and feel very light on my feet. I had the thought that these voices were from God and that he was trying to tell me something. I also had the thought that I was to build an investment firm and help out others with the proceeds, thereby helping the world. I had been religiously reading the Wall Street Journal and therefore was not short on ideas about where the market was headed. My plan was to sell notes for various maturities at about a ten percent interest rate. I thought that since nobody expected the market to do better than ten percent, on average, I could beat the market and pocket the difference. After careful analysis I came up with the theory that the stock market would drop by fifty percent within the next three or four months; my theory came, came in part, by noticing that home foreclosures were up in a small Wall Street Journal article. The theory of mine preceded the mortgage crises in 2008, so I was spot on; unfortunately the crash took a little longer to take place than I expected and also my Bi-Polar caused all of my carefully orchestrated plans to unravel miserably.

To plan for the coming crash I wrote an article about how Finance executives were using as much financial leverage as possible to jack up returns, while the very foundation of financial instruments, especially Mortgage Backed Securities was shaky. The instability came from the fact that mortgage borrowers were having trouble making payments and due to high debt levels of borrowers it was only getting worse. Once the stream of mortgage money slowed down, by foreclosures, the instruments that are based on the mortgages, called Mortgage Backed Securities, would unravel causing a stock market crash. After I finished the article I decided to swing by my alma mater and distribute my doom and gloom on the stock market. I also dropped off a flyer at my aunt and uncles house, and swung by a local company, Prairie Electric, and talked to the CFO about my fears of a stock market crash.

In addition, I planned to incorporate the students at Clark College with my new company, Wirtanen Investments. I swung by Clark College a few times, wanting to talk to the president of the college about my plans. Finally, one day while I was at Clark College some of the security personnel surrounded me and asked me what I was doing. They also searched my bag and in it I had a mini computer which was cutting edge technology at the time; the computer had cost around $2500 dollars. When the security woman saw the computer she gently put it back and they left me alone.

To capitalize on the coming crash, I decided to buy puts which are the option to sell a stock at a predetermined price. By buying the puts, I would make a killing if the stock market dropped by fifty percent or more. I also entered the futures market, by buying some gold and some options for milk. The milk options were bought because I read about a drought in Australia, which has a lot of dairy farms. I thought the lack of good feed would cause the units of milk to decline and the price to go up. The problem was that I had little experience in futures and options trading, and because of being manic, I was trying to do too many things too quickly. I misread the way that the put options on the Dow Jones Industrial Average were quoted and instead of spending three hundred dollars on puts, at fifty cents apiece, I spent three thousand dollars, at five dollars apiece. Because I did not have three thousand cash in my account the trading platform automatically sold out of my other positions, some at gains and some at losses, leaving me a net loss of eleven hundred dollars. Instead of becoming rich with a crash in the Dow I became poor, but that was only the beginning.

Bipolar can be hard on the finances, as well as on relationships, and on how smoothly life goes in general. A girl and I had dated when I was around nineteen and because I planned to go to school we called off the dating and decided to wait until I graduated from college. When I graduated from school and the weekend after my first transcendental experience and the interview with Fisher Investments, she decided to make a trip to Washington State to see if I was still interested in her. I saw her in the food line at church but was not sure if now was the time to propose to her, so I literally waited on a sign from God. Because I did not receive a sign from God, I decided not to talk to her until I received a sign. She then left to go back to Kalispell, Montana and I found out later that she had been talking to my friends about how we were going to get married. She must have been furious when she traveled all the way out to Washington and I was not able to talk to her, because I did not receive a sign from God.

A day or two after she left, I felt compelled to send her an e-mail letting her know that I wanted to talk to her. She replied, "it would be better that you would never think of me again." Not taking rejection so easily, I decided to take a trip to Kalispell and have her say that to my face. I hopped into my somewhat sporty Volkswagen Jetta and armed with her address, began my journey at top speed. Being in a manic state of mind, speed was essential. My car governed out at 120 mph and I governed it out numerous times. Through the mountain passes I drove like a racecar driver, crouched over the wheel as cars moved aside for me. I imagined that there would be people after me in the future as I would have a lot of money and I needed to practice. After cornering at over double the suggested speed, I decided that the vehicle was cornering so well, that God must be holding it to the road. Since God was holding it to the road, I decided to test out how fast I could go with the help of God. I went faster and faster, burning through record amounts of gas. Just after St. Regis, Montana, I was going around a corner, with some whoops, at 110 miles an hour and I lost control. I remember feeling totally relaxed as I spun and slid backwards at 110 miles an hour. I then rolled and flipped and ended up back on the road with every facet of the car being smashed except where I was sitting, after looking at the car it was a miracle that I survived. I hopped out of the car unhurt, with some minor rug burns and a scrape. I remember thinking that God must not have liked my car, because it was a little too flashy.

After an ambulance showed up, I was transported to a local Montana Hospital and checked out. The transportation by ambulance was required, because the car had flipped. When I arrived at the hospital, and after being checked out, I had the thought that now was the time to see if the girl I still loved had any feelings for me at all. If she would agree to come pick me up from the hospital, maybe she still cared a little. After all, I would agree to pick up almost anybody from the hospital if they had gotten in an accident, regardless if I cared about them or not. I gave her parents a call because that was the only number I had and asked her mom if Susan was home. Susan was not home but her mom agreed to ask her if she would come pick me up. I talked to her mom a little while later and she said that there was no way that Susan would come and get me. She did say that she and Jim would come get me if I needed a ride. My test of Susan completed, so far, I said I would take care of finding a ride on my own. I called up my Godfather Chris, who lives in Kalispell and he agreed to come and get me and said that I could spend some time at their place.

My time in Kalispell was a dream, I felt very close to God and heaven, I was completely happy, except I still wanted to talk to Susan face to face. I drove around Chris and Becky's van and went shooting with Chris. The weather was nice and sunny, early summer weather. That Sunday I talked to Susan in the basement at church and she verified, face to face, that she had no feelings for me. I then went and talked to a pastor about my situation and he said that, while it was tough, if she had no feelings; there was nothing to be done. I left the church with my head spinning, feeling completely lost.

Given that she had rejected me, I planned my return trip home. Because I had no vehicle I decided to take the train. Before I left, I thought of another girl I knew who had shown some interest in me, Sarah. I felt that it was a good idea if I moved on to the next opportunity, to ease the pain. I called up my cousin Bethany, a friend of Sarah's, and asked her for Sarah's number. She happily gave it to me and asked if I wanted to know anything about Sarah. I was so confident in Sarah that I declined any information and got right down to the business of sending her a text message. On the train ride home, I gazed at the beautiful scenery and wrote to Sarah about how beautiful the train ride home was. The train ride was through the afternoon and night. When we took off about 4 p.m. the seat next to me was empty and when it began to get dark I went to sleep. About 2 or 3 in the morning I woke up to a younger girl, maybe legal age, curled up next to me with her back pressed to mine. In my delusional state I imagined that she had been sent to me by the Catholic Church to tempt me into falling away from my faith, Old Apostolic Lutheran. When the train ride was over, I penned her a short note inviting her to my church, in hopes that she would convert and that this would give me another option.

The next weekend, I borrowed my dad's pickup and went to a get together at Sarah's house. She was dressed for success, and I could tell she was excited to see me. Once again though, instead of just going talk to her, I decided to play it cool and observe. She was nervous and smoked multiple cigarettes. I could tell she wanted me to talk to her and was smoking to burn off some tension. Finally, it all came to a head on a Sunday. I was talking in a group of my friends and she came up behind me with her friend, like they wanted me to talk to her. I once again declined to talk, opting to test if she truly cared. Doesn't make sense to a rational mind but I thought that a little test wouldn't hurt her. She became angry and when I texted her later, she said she wanted nothing to do with me.

With Sarah out of the way, I was becoming desperate. One day I was hanging out with my buddy Matt, at Starbucks and I got the feeling that if I didn't marry soon I would burn in hell. Desperate I ran out of Starbucks and asked the first girl I saw out on a date. She told me that she was too young to date.

My thoughts continued to get more and more delusional and while I had some wonderful feelings, I also had terrible delusions that caused me to panic. For example, I thought that the city of Battle Ground was going to be destroyed because Christian girls were wearing pants. Women are recommended to wear dresses in my faith. I became so convinced that the city would be destroyed, that I was determined to flee town.

I took off for California in my Hyundai Accent one evening, where I thought I would be safe. Driving away I had a feeling that God was with me and I felt powerful. I had this powerful feeling earlier as well, as part of my delusional experiences. One day everything seemed to fall together orderly and perfectly, then when I hopped in my car and drove, it felt like a tank. I thought that this new sense of power was a gift that I had gotten upon my successful completion and graduation of college. Along with these delusions, I could live off of very little food and I lost weight rapidly. I exercised immensely and one day survived all day on a little fruit juice and a piece of chicken. I felt very full from this piece of chicken and could not even eat it all. It felt very heavy and filling, as did the fruit juice. I remember thinking that this was how Jesus fed the multitude on three loaves and two fishes.

I did not make it to California, because I drove the wrong way and my car broke down. I ended up in a small town in the Columbia River Gorge. I slept in the back of my car and then jogged to the nearest farm to look for help with my car. I remember thinking how peaceful the farm looked and thinking this might be a little like heaven. Then when I asked the farmer for help, he called the police. The police brought me back to my car and helped me call a tow truck. He also directed me to California, with a map. I was way out of the way to go to California.

My brother came and picked me up, after I had chilled out for a while in the park in the nearest town. I was ravenous, and subsided on a little popcorn and a bottle of pop. I asked some people that were barbecuing for some food and they declined to give me any. I imagined that this would have been a chance for them to help out one of God's little ones and help their path to heaven but since they declined, they would be going to hell. Also, in that town, I just missed hopping the freight to get out of town; I was a little too slow.

Back at home, I was in a panic to get away because I still believed Battleground would be destroyed, even if I had to walk. Before I left though, I wanted to get all of my guns, so I would have some protection in California. Unfortunately, my parents had raided my room and taken all of my guns and hid them, because of my erratic behavior. Also unfortunately, they had neglected to find my 22 pistol, and I left with that to seek the return of my possessions. My dad, seeing me with a gun tried to tackle me and the gun went off in the ground.

11 CLARK COUNTY JAIL

Six or eight police cars pulled up and the officers all crouched around their cars with guns drawn. I calmly walked out with my hands in the air and my pants full of shit from the struggle that had just finished up in the house. I unfortunately was out of my mind and had been trying to leave home to go to California. I also thought my family was going to kill me, so I had a 22 pistol to protect myself. My dad, seeing me with a gun in the house, and fearing the worst, tried to take it away from me. In the ensuing struggle, someone dialed 911.

Just as I entered the cop car, I remember thinking I am Jesus Christ because Jesus's walk was too perfect for mankind to follow and mine was sinful enough that if a person tried they could follow it. I then had the thought that I should say nothing to any questions asked. At the time, I could hear a voice and I believed that voice to be God, in other words, I was unmedicated and undiagnosed, but later on would be diagnosed with bipolar one with psychotic features. The psychotic features led to the voices.

What is your name, they asked at intake to the Clark County Jail? I gave no reply and did not answer anything else. They then gave me an Orange Jumpsuit, which meant a violent offender, and put me in a cell with another inmate. Being in the quite like that I quickly became paranoid and thought that my brother and dad were coming to kill me because in my delusional state of mind I believed they were jealous of me because I was going to heaven and they were going to hell. Why I believed they were going to Hell is difficult to explain.

For some reason, maybe because I started screaming, I was moved to solitary and then the true Hell began for me. After being in a solitary cell for a while I began to believe that the world had ended and that this was my hell forever. At first I just believed that they had placed me in the cell by accident because I was not guilty of anything. I would explain to them that I was not guilty and they would tell me that I was. I just did not understand what I had done to deserve being put in that cell. Yes I had a pistol and I had pointed it at my mother, but when she asked me to put it down, I immediately did so. To me everything had just gotten blown out of proportion and I had never intended to do anything wrong. After many times of explaining I was innocent and should be released from the cell, I truly began to believe I would never be released and that this was my Hell. In fact, I even saw scratched out drawings on the walls of the cell and believed they meant different things. For example, there were the words Cain and Abel on the door of the cell and I believed that I was Cain and that was why I had ended up in this hell. Every day I would holler and pound on the steel door with the flats of my hands. If the guards would tire of my pounding, they would move me to another cell. One time they moved me to a padded room and then I quit pounding and passed out, pounding is futile in a rubber room. All the time in solitary I was dressed in a green suicide smock. Some of the time my smock would come off and I would be naked with cold air blowing from the vent.

Part of the time I was suicidal but there was no way to kill myself, I tried to flush my head down the toilet one time but that was a failure. For a while I was sent to suicide watch, where they watch if you are going to commit suicide. While I was there the guards decided to move me to another cell. They marched in and told me to put my hands against the wall, not wanting to leave my bible behind I leaned over and reached for it; the guards thought I was resisting them and threw me down on the ground and tased me. They also used a steel bar to pry my hands behind my back. My wrist became hurt and I was bleeding from my forehead, from where it hit the concrete. They sent me to the hospital to get my face stitched up, and then I returned to jail. While at the hospital I was shackled with three shackles to the hospital bed, one hand was free; a women watched while I peed in a cup and I remember thinking that it was Angelina Jolie. I also saw a nurse I knew from the church I go to and I thought she was a captive at the hospital, which was kind of like a Hell.

After a while I believed the food was poisoned and I quit eating. I also would get letters from my mother but I believed her and her sisters were witches and they were jealous of my power, so they wanted to haunt me. I would even feel little prickles on my fingers if I would try to read the letters from my mother, so I flushed them all down the toilet. One day I was hungry enough so I decided to try an apple. After taking a bite I felt like I started stretching, so I threw that in the toilet too. At its worst, I could actually here the Christians going to Heaven in a giant spaceship and I was being left behind forever. I was ready to beat my head against the wall, but at that moment I remembered, where there is life there is hope. After remembering those words from somewhere, I began to realize that I was actually still alive so I was not really in hell. Shortly thereafter I was transferred to Western State Mental Hospital; it had been one horrible hellish month in solitary. One takeaway from that experience is that when you truly believe in eternity without God, as I do, that is head spinning and suicidal crazy.

I spent a month in jail and three months at Western State Mental hospital. The charges were dropped to Aiming or Discharge of a Firearm and I was released stable and on Lithium. I was diagnosed with Bi-Polar One with psychotic features.

The three months at Western State went pretty smooth. At Western State, I became stable in a week or two, on Zyprexa, and then spent a lot of time playing ping pong. I also got a lot of visitors, even though it was a two hour drive to where I was. I remember thinking that when I arrived at Western State, that this was a Roman Catholic Church sanctuary and that they were taking care of me because I was beautiful. Some of the answers I gave the staff were real off the wall. For example, they asked me if I

was married and I said I was married to Angelina Jolie. They then asked me, what happened to Brad Pitt, I was not sure. While the three months at Western State were bearable, the one month in the Clark County Jail was hell. I was in solitary the entire time with nothing to wear but a green suicide smock. Part of the time I was on suicide watch, because I told the nurse I tried to drown myself in the toilet; most of the time while I was there, I believed that the world was over and that this was my own personal hell. I would pound on the cell door in hopes to be released and say that I was not supposed to be locked up. Every once in a while they would tire of me beating on the door and would switch me to another cell or a padded room. Cold air would blow through the vent and I did not know how to put on my smock part of the time, so I would be entirely naked. Also the food was disgusting and I thought it was poisoned. Huge piles of food would build up and I would just lay there and stagnate. One day the guards wanted to move me from suicide watch to another cell and five of them came in my cell to move me. The guards told me to get up and put my hands against the wall, not wanting to leave my bible behind I leaned over and reached for it; the guards thought I was resisting them and threw me down on the ground and tased me. They also used a steel bar to pry my hands behind my back. My wrist became hurt and I was bleeding from my forehead, from where it hit the concrete. They sent me to the hospital to get my face stitched up, and then I returned to jail. While at the hospital I was shackled with three shackles to the hospital bed, one hand was free; a women watched while I peed in a cup and I remember thinking that it was Angelina Jolie. I also saw a nurse I knew from the church I go to and I thought she was a captive at the hospital, which was kind of like a Hell. Finally, when I was about to beat my head against the wall, in the jail cell, I realized I was still alive and that where there is life there is hope. At that point it became a little better because I did not any longer believe entirely that that was my eternity.

12 GOOD FEELINGS

Before I entered the Clark County Jail, were some of the best feeling days of my life. I would wake up early, around three or four in the morning, without an alarm clock, and would just lay there for an hour or so listening to the birds chirp. At some times the colors seemed much brighter and everything seemed slowed down. At one point when I was watching a hummingbird at a feeder, its wings appeared to be moving so slow that I could see them. Animals also did not appear to be scared of me and I got very close to a deer once or twice. I remember thinking that this was a foretaste of what heaven would be like, it was truly amazing.

While I was not just enjoying my surroundings I would be reading the Wall street Journal, Forbes, and other investment magazines and newspapers, to try to come up with the next things to invest in. In addition, I kept thinking about what would happen in the future and how God would help reveal this, since I believed I was talking with God.

One day I took a trip to Barnes and Nobel's and just started picking books up off the shelf based on a prick I would feel in my heart. In other words when I ran my finger over the spine of a book if I felt a small prick in my heart I would select the book. I ended up with a stack of books selected this way and took them home.

When I came home I found one book on military training and used this book as motivation to begin training, running up hills and eating less, for a time when I would need to lead the Christians away from persecution. During this manic time I had boundless energy. As you can tell there is a number of things going on as my mind was always racing and coming up with ideas which I would then pursue. Unfortunately, I tried to pursue every idea that came into my head and that lead to trouble and helped ensure that Wirtanen Investments Corporation would never get off the ground.

As I mentioned earlier I spent a lot of time reading the Wall Street, and while reading it I stumbled upon a small article that said that home foreclosures were going up; I used this information alongside what I already knew about Mortgage Backed Securities, to develop a theory that the stock market was going to drop by fifty percent. I then planned on using this predication as a catalyst to build my company when it came true. In addition, I planned on buying "puts" the option to sell the market at a predetermined price that would profit if the market did indeed drop by fifty percent.

Many days I would publicize the coming crash and the need to pull your money out of the stock market for a short time until the market did drop. Actually, three or four months later the market did drop and we had the 2008 mortgage crisis, I was spot on, but too crazy to take advantage of it. Had I been of a sound mind I would have profited off of the put options and then used that money to invest into the next solid opportunity.

After I regained my stability, I moved into a trailer at my Grandma and Grandpas and began looking for work. I found work for my cousin Marlon doing concrete work and this helped pay expenses, while I continued to look for work doing something related to my schooling. One of the individuals I worked with when working for Marlon had done quite a lot of hallucinogenic drugs and when I told him about my experiences while manic and psychotic, he told me that many people pay for the experiences I had.

I had accumulated a bit of debt while manic, but fortunately my sister had returned a lot of the possessions I bought, like a fancy wardrobe from Pac Sun and Buckle. I had been very proud of my new image, so I was a little disappointed when I heard that my sister had returned everything, even though it saved me money in the end. Unfortunately my $2500 dollar minicomputer could not be returned and it was not worth much if sold.

13 MANIC

At first when I am getting manic it is manageable. I sleep less, function faster, and am more creative; all of these traits have helped me out when accomplishing tasks like winning the Gonzaga Business Plan Competition. However, as time goes on and I continue to function on three or so hours of sleep a night the mania turns into delusional thinking and I even hallucinate. In addition to the hallucinations I become unable to complete anything as my mind races from task to task. The hallucinations that I experience are very real; in fact, they are as real as if they actually happened. This can lead me to be confused about what is real and what is not real and if something happened that is way out there, I tended to keep it to myself because I knew that other people would believe I was going crazy if I mentioned what I had experienced. Some of the hallucinations I experienced are as follows:

While driving my Volkswagen Jetta at one point the car felt like a tank and rumbled when I drove down the road, then when I accelerated and cornered it felt like God was holding my car to the rode. The tires positively stuck to the pavement and I cornered at double or triple the suggested speed limits. At another point I was talking to a police officer and he wanted my license, I gave it to him and when he gave it back to me it was not a license anymore, but a wood knitting needle. I was surprised to receive a wood knitting needle instead of my license and I handled it for a while and determined that it was indeed a knitting needle, I then put it in my pocket and it disappeared. To account for this occurrence I determined that it was the Devil playing tricks on me. At another time I would feel very full off of a small amount of food like a piece of chicken and half a bottle of fruit juice. At first I thought this was how Jesus fed the multitude but after further reading in the bible, later on, I noticed that there were many baskets of fragments left over from the meal that Jesus blessed, which would make my theory of only feeling full, and the food feeling heavier not true. On another occasion I watched a hummingbird and could actually see its wings going up and down as if everything was in slow motion, also right around this time I walked up to a deer and almost touched it. Finally, when I was in the Clark County jail for an extended period of time the cold water in the tap turned to hot water. This was after I had felt the water for many weeks and it had always been cold. Then all of a sudden the water was hot, so I cleaned myself off with it. Also, in the Clark County Jail after I had been screaming and hollering for hours I saw the back of a large scaly lizard in a reflective part of the wall. As a side note, if I was not screaming or hollering that I should be released, I would be singing Jesus Loves me, or rambling on about something that did not make sense.

In my delusional state of mind I believed all of the things that I saw that were not explainable to be the work of the devil or of God.

14 BOB AND RUTH'S

When I got out of Clark county jail I could not live at home because there was a restraining order against me having to do with my mom. My mom did not put the restraining order in place but the firearm incident had been labeled as domestic violence and an automatic restraining order had been put into place. This restraining order was horrible for my mother because she was not allowed to see me. For me it was not that big of a deal to not be able to go home because I had just spent months locked up and would have been happy living on the street.

 Since I could not live at home my dad and I used some money that had been donated from my friends to buy a small travel trailer that I could live in. My friends were very generous during my first breakdown and donated thousands of dollars to help pay for expenses, such as legal costs. They also wrote many letters of support.

At my grandma and grandpas we parked the trailer and I found it stocked with food along with fifty dollars in cash that would help me buy a few things until I started working for my cousin John, doing flatwork, later on. Life was good at my grandma and grandpas, as I had a good relationship with them that only got better.

Why I ended up in a trailer I am not sure. Perhaps my grandma and grandpa felt more comfortable with me having my own place, as they did not know how long I would be living there. I personally did not care where I lived as I was just happy to be out of jail. It so happens that my cousin John bought my Grandma and Grandpas place after their death and the trailer is parked there undercover. My cousin John did some brick work on a sauna at my mom and dad's place and my dad, sick of the trailer sitting around and taking up space traded it for the work. I guess you could consider it my donation for the sauna, as I now enjoy a sauna two to three times a week.

Most days at Bob and Ruth's I would work for three or four hours for my cousin Marlon and then hangout at Grandma and Grandpas. At Grandma and Grandpas I would go on jogs and lift weights. In the evenings I would spend time visiting with my Grandma and Grandpa and my cousin Eric from Norway who was an exchange student. Eric got in a bad auto accident later on and almost died. None of us knew if he would ever be the same again, when it looked like he would survive, and I felt fortunate to have spent time with him when I had the chance.

Working for my cousin Marlon was great. It was good exercise and my cousin was very relaxed. I worked doing concrete work which can be very physical. This type of physical work can be just the thing for me when I am healing from a manic break as I was. The work does not task the mind much but it is good exercise on the body. Now I am doing bookkeeping which does not task the body physically, but I go to the gym and work out for an hour or so a day for my mental and physical health. Working for Marlon I also got to work with some interesting characters such as one former drug user who when I told him about my psychotic experiences told me that people pay money for trips like that. He was a very happy go lucky fellow and was sure I would end up working for Fisher Investments and driving a Mercedes with gold spinners yet.

Even though I was working for my cousin doing flatwork, a type of concrete work involving pouring concrete slabs, I started to get fat and hit 240 pounds at one point. Unfortunately the medication that I was on Zyprexa has a side effect of weight gain, later on I would be switched to Lithium. A big part of why I got fat was because I ate so much. I would wake up in the middle of the night ravenous and would eat half a block of mozzarella cheese and a pack of soda crackers. After hitting 240 though I put a stop to my midnight eating and upped my exercise program. After a while on this new diet I lost ten pounds.

After a few months at my grandma and grandpas we were able to get the restraining order dropped and I moved back home. It was great to be back home and to see the family again, but as I mentioned before, I was happy under any circumstance because I had just come out of months of solitary confinement. I have great memories of my grandma and grandpa, who are now dead, because of the time I spent at their house visiting with them, watching my grandpa run an excavator, split wood, have his morning coffee etc.

15 STATE AUDITOR

The following April I interviewed with a number of different places, including the Washington State Attorney General's Office, and the Washington State Auditor's Office. Both places liked me, but the Auditor's Office seemed most promising, so I took that. They must not have done a background check or if they did, my references were good enough.

For the first year to year and a half I excelled at the Auditor's Office. In fact, during a performance review my supervisor Roger said, "if we had asked you to walk on water, you could have done it." About a year and a half later though, my lithium level was probably getting a little low, or else I needed an anti-psychotic, because I had another breakdown. One morning I woke up, in Olympia, and was not able to move. It felt like my housemates were devils and when they tried to feed me something, the bread got stuck in my throat. They told me not to go anywhere and that they would try to call for help, but I was panicked because I thought they were devils and I took off for home. Back at home I was committed into a mental hospital to be evaluated, but they did not find the right medication or dosage. Below me and in the hallway I heard very heavy footsteps and I quickly developed the idea that the Smiths were devils and that they were in Hell already. I dared not move and before too long Mrs. Smith called out if I was going to work today. I was working at the Washington State Auditor's Office in Olympia and I had been living with the

Smith's for around a year now. This would be my second breakdown, in my battle with bipolar disorder. Leading up to the breakdown it had been difficult for me to sleep and I had been taking a sleeping pill every night to go along with the small dose of lithium I had been prescribed, around 500 milligrams a day.

Mr. Smith came into the room and I could not physically get out of bed, so he carried me downstairs and offered me some bread. I tried to eat it but started chocking on it, so Mr. Smith called 911 and asked for help. Mr. and Mrs. Smith and their son Kevin all had to leave for work, so Mr. Smith told me not to go anywhere and that help would arrive soon. As soon as they left though I panicked, because I still thought they were devils, and I walked out to my car, started it up, and headed for home. I remember driving down the freeway and thinking that the Semis were much larger than normal, I was hallucinating.

A few hours later I arrived home, at my mom and dads, and I explained a little about what had happened. They called up one of our church pastors and a nurse that was a friend of mine, to come talk to me. After I talked to both of them for a while someone determined I needed professional help and dialed 911. I did not know that anyone had been called though, so I went into my room and started ranting and raving at the wall. I then curled up in a ball on my bed and a little while later an ambulance showed up and dragged me against my will to the hospital.

At the hospital I was placed in a small room and after the psychiatrist evaluated me, it was determined that I would go to station two section nine. However, there was a long wait to get into the mental hospital and so I was placed in a room in the upstairs of the hospital and unusually enough, I was allowed to wander anywhere in the hospital I would like, while I was stark raving mad. I would do commando rolls on the floor and one time I even walked out of the hospital and went for a little walk.

A few weeks later a bed opened up at Station two and I was admitted to the mental hospital. I was then at the hospital for about three more weeks and I was delusional the entire time. The doctor tried a variety of medications to stabilize me but every one of them seemed to have side effects as well as it did not work to cure my mania.

While at station two there was a big guy with a shaved head that liked to patrol the hallways. In my delusional state of mind I believed he was a member of the Special Forces that was being rehabilitated and that he was very dangerous. I feared to walk the hallways and I also feared to go asleep because I thought he would come into my bedroom and kill me. I was awake for around eleven straight days while at the mental hospital, and I defiantly was not losing my mania.

Even though I lived in fear, part of the time at station two was enjoyable. There was a beautiful intern from a local college that would visit with me and play board games with me. We would also have art classes where I would build things out of leather and also draw pictures.

The entire time I was there I was delusional and I believed I was in a special training camp to be in the Special Forces. Each of the patients had a different role and some of the staff did too; for example, Brandy a pretty brunette, liked to flirt with me and was an undercover FBI agent.

After two or three weeks I was released from station two still suffering from delusions. I had been able to answer all of the questions correctly for them to release me, but I was far from well. Back at home for a few days, I had had such a good time at the mental hospital, I decided that I needed to go back. Mostly I missed the girls.

When I arrived back at station two some of the people I had gotten to know in the prior two weeks had left and new ones had arrived. Katie had left to go back to school, which made me unhappy. However, a student from Clark College named Mary had arrived. Mary was actually a patient as I believe she had been suicidal. In the next two weeks I got to know Mary real well and as I was a little older than her, I believe she looked up to me. Fortunately, the guy with the shaved head had left, so I was no longer in fear.

After a few weeks I left Station Two again, still delusional. I had gotten Mary's email from a friend of hers and a while after I got out I tried to email her, she never replied. Years later I saw her and a few of her friends at a skate park and she looked sick to her stomach when she saw me, I'm not sure what that was all about, but hopefully her life has went well.

After the second time I got out everyone assumed I was doing fine, but I was actually still very delusional and believed that the government was watching me. I did however function well enough to rent an apartment and I rented a nice apartment and went back to work. At work I simply could not concentrate or function and while not at work I led a very interesting lifestyle.

I would pull down the shades in my apartment and exercise in the nude. It just felt so free being nude that I just kept the shades down and half the time I did not even dress. I was seriously manic so for about three months straight I got no more than three hours of sleep every night; this gave me plenty of time to pursue other things but work.

A big staple in my routine was music videos and pornography. I had not seen a naked woman until my second breakdown, when I was around twenty five, or listened to any music videos, so this style of life was all new and fresh to me. I loved Lady Gaga music videos as well as Ozzie, Hannah Montana, and Britany Spears. Hannah Montana was very popular at the time and I actually thought she was an angel sent down from heaven, her voice was so beautiful.

If I was not listening to music videos I was scaring the grandma lady next door by rubbing knives on the stove burners and making sex moans, going out for a late night drive in my Subaru Legacy Wagon, practicing commando rolls in the yard, scaling a McDonalds fence with bare feet in the dark, or intimidating people by revving the engine on my Subaru and pretending I was going to run them over. I did this because I thought I was a gang boss and these were members of a rival gang that needed to be culled into the herd. One night I did a big loop all the way from Olympia to Mount Rainier and back and made it to work on time the next morning. Another night I skateboarded in the Safeway parking lot at about two in the morning; the police finally showed up and told me I should go back home.

At some point during it all I thought that God wanted me to buy a Ninja Super Sport 650. I bought a Ninja for $6,500 dollars and along came more trouble. Driving the Ninja up and down the highway at around 120 mph to 130 mph, I was eventually caught and thrown into jail for the weekend. Fortunately I kept my job thorough it all as I still worked at the auditor's office for a while after I was done being manic.

Finally after three months of mania I was curled up in a ball in my room in a fetal position and unable to function. I was getting ready to hit the depressive side of bipolar. My mom and two brothers came up to Olympia to try to get me to come home with them because I was being evicted from my apartment for too many 911 calls. Being paranoid I would not accept their help. Instead I called the police because I got sick of them being around and disturbing me.

The police showed up and I answered the door naked to ensure that they knew that I did not have a gun. At the time I believed there were satellites watching my every move as well as recording devices hid in my apartment. After the police asked me a few questions I went to sit on the couch and tilted my head sideways and zoned out. They then decided to transport me to the hospital as I had answered the door naked and this proved that I was truly crazy.

At the hospital I got bored in the room they gave me and I started mooning the cameras. I decided that since they were watching me I may as well put on a show. They then decided I would be sent to a mental hospital in Olympia, where I would finally get stabilized.

After I was stable I suffered with depression for three months. The three months of mania had worn me out so bad that I could do almost nothing and could definitely not work. Depression was so bad I was in bed most of the time and it was a real effort to even move. I thought of suicide many times but never actually came up with a plan to do it.

After I was well enough to return to work it was time to deal with the motorcycle incident. While it had been the time of my life to weave in and out of traffic at 120 or so mph I would now pay the piper for having failed to see the officer of the law who was behind me for six miles.

I had been out on bail and was charged with Felony Allude, Reckless driving. The Felony carried a max sentence of a year in prison. I hired a good attorney who billed out at about $350 dollars an hour but when I met with him he did not have much hope of beating the rap. He said that even though I did not see the officer of the law behind me, the officer was saying I turned my head back multiple times and did see him. He also said the officer's word is what will usually stand and that we would have to try a different tact.

After the attorney learned that I had been out of my mind during the entire incident and had a history of mental illness, he felt that we should try for a Not Guilty By Reason of Insanity. He was able to get two doctors in psychiatry from Western State Mental Hospital to evaluate me and after their evaluation they determined that I met the definition of legally insane when I had been driving the motorcycle. A big part of the reason for that decision was that I had been delusional at the time and truly believed that I was being followed by the government and that they did not mind if I sped.

The judge hearing the professional's opinion decided to grant me a NGRI as long as I was supervised by the department of corrections for a period of five years. This was an unusual decision in that I did not have to spend any time at Western State Mental hospital because the Doctors had determined that I was now sane and did not pose a threat to the public. Normally when you get a NRGI you can spend years at western state until they determine you are safe to return to the public.

Back at work I was put on an easier assignment because I was still somewhat depressed and could not concentrate at my full ability. I wanted to quit because it was so hard to work while depressed but I kept at it. The doctors at the Olympia hospital had put me on a few milligrams of Risperidone and on a higher dose of Lithium. However, when I tried to do more complex tasks at work I had trouble and the doctor I was working with and I determined that the cause was the Risperidone. The doctor decided to lower the risperidone until it was just therapeutic and eventually get rid of it all together. This proved to be a mistake as I have now been functioning well on two milligrams of Risperidone. The doctor lowered the Risperidone to .5 mg and it was probably too low to keep me from going psychotic again and suffering my third breakdown.

After getting a choice of either losing my job with the State Auditor's Office or transferring to Spokane to be a Financial Statement Auditor, I chose to transfer to Spokane. Near Spokane, is a small town called Davenport, WA and in Davenport is a locality of Christians that practice the same faith as I do. Because I had more friends in Davenport I chose to initially rent there even though I would have about an hour drive to work, depending on where we were working. As a Financial Statement Auditor you go to the place you are going to audit and are rarely at the home office. This is unlike what I was used to as an IT Auditor we would spend a lot of time writing code to search databases for information that would lead to Audit teams going out and auditing based on our findings. Sometime as an IT auditor we would go to the auditee's location, but probably over half the time was spent at the office.

As a Financial Statement Auditor we would go to places like Pend

Oreille County WA, Liberty Lake Washington and many other small or big towns. On one occasion I spent time auditing my alma mater WSU, on another occasion we audited a courthouse, at another time a landfill. Every morning we would carpool, often in the assistant manager's Escalade, where she would listen to non-stop techno...lame. I actually enjoyed my time Financial Statement Auditing and I got along well with the team. However, I could not keep up with the pace of the work. The new work that I was doing had much smaller budgets then I was used to and I was consistently twenty percent over budget. Finally after talking with HR and the director it was decided that my illness could be causing me to work slower, but that the audit team did not have the budget to reasonably accommodate me under the American's with Disabilities act. I received a Disability Separation.

Even though I got laid off though I do not regret making the move to Spokane, I have many good memories of living independently for nine months and spending time mountain biking in the countryside of Davenport, visiting church friends some evenings, and taking Brazilian Jiu Jitsu at a local studio after I moved from Davenport to Spokane. While I was in Spokane my friend from Church Glen, was working out of town on an electrical job and I have fond memories of going for evening jogs with him. Much of life for me is just slivers of time where I get to meet different people and do different things for a short period of time until I move on to the next adventure.

16 Third Breakdown

I decided to start my unemployment with a vacation and I took a road trip to Vanderhoof Canada to visit my sister. I then traveled home and took off for Finland to go to my friend's wedding. The wedding was a typical beautiful long Finnish wedding. In Finland I was beginning to slip again but I was stable enough my entire trip that nobody could tell. When I got home I took my new dirt bike for a few spins and went to my brother's wedding in Minneapolis.

When I got back home from Minneapolis, I totally slipped into delusions again, starting with a midnight drive to Camas. When I was driving I became lost and thought I was driving to a new heaven and a new earth. It is likely that my dosage of antipsychotic became too low because I was working with the doctor to lower it, so I could better function at work. I finally arrived at a park after midnight and tried to sleep in my car. I had not a clue where I was, I thought that I was in a new heaven and a new earth and I that I needed to explore it. In the morning I got out of my car and walked to the nearest house. I thought that this house could be mine, if I just walked in and took possession of it. Unfortunately, the door was locked; also unfortunately, when I walked to the backdoor it was open.

I walked right into the house and took possession, nobody was home. I was very tired so I crawled into the nearest bed I saw and went to bed, after spraying some girlie spray under the covers to make it smell better. I woke up to paramedics doing chest compressions on me and wanting to know if I had taken anything. I told them I had taken ecstasy, because I thought they would treat me better if they thought I was rich enough to afford that.

I ended up being charged with Residential Burglary, which got dropped to Criminal Trespass. I spent some more time in the Clark County Jail and in the process met a cool guy, who probably also had Bi-Polar, by the name of Major Tony Michael Holland. He claimed he was very rich and I bought it all. He gave me a list of things to go see, where people would know him, including the Lewis River Golf Course. When I got out I took a trip to the Lewis River Golf Course and had a good meal, followed with a cigar.

Still out of my mind I enrolled at Clark College to take some computer classes, but could not concentrate on the course work. On one quiz I wrote that I was with the Mafia and was only taking classes for the fun of it. I quit my classes at Clark and decided that I wanted to learn more about the Mafia.

As a cover for learning about the Mafia, I came up with the idea that I was working on my Doctorates in Economic Geography. Since a big part of the economy is the underworld, such as the drug industry, parts of the skin trade, etc. I would need to frequent establishments that had individuals involved in these types of activities. In my delusional mind I would often notice things that I would believe were signs, which would lead me to go certain places or do certain things. For example, I would get ideas such as Portland has a rose on many of its signs and the rose stands for Mafia therefore a good place to learn about the Mafia is in Portland. Since the Mafia has been reputed to be involved with all the shady industries such as gambling and the skin trade, I decided to find them by going clubbing, specifically strip clubbing. I was unemployed at the time and making about 1200 dollars a month on unemployment, so I had no shortage of money to go clubbing with.

My first night of clubbing was exciting. I drove to Stump Town Coffee and parked my car. I then walked down the street and asked someone where I could find a strip club. The he-she, male dressed as a female, told me he could direct me to one and led me to a club. After paying the money to get in I found out it was a theater with porn on the big screen. I chilled out there for a while, but feeling ripped off I left and eventually found my first strip club. The first club I entered was one that was good for 18 and over, so they did not serve alcohol. I bought some Martinnelie's sparkling cider and sipped it with the stripper out of plastic wineglasses. That was all good but I wanted some more action, so I wandered down the street to a real club, Club Rouge. I paid the five dollars coverage and wandered in with about 150 dollars to make it rain. One of the strippers on the pole looked lonely and forlorn and the other two were not doing much, so I started ordering up lap dances. I started with the lonely looking one and then moved to the other two to be fair. They were all excited after the lap dances and began to put on quite a show. I was free with the fives and twenties and that probably helped as well. I saw one tight older man slide across an extra dollar after the stripper that was lonely got warmed up and introduced herself to him. Finally I was down to my last three dollars, with no plans to head to an ATM. One of the girls asked me if I wanted another lap dance, so I said I had only three dollars to my name. She said that would be fine and gave me that lap dance right out in front for all to see.

Another night, I drove down to Portland and parked near the flashing lights. I walked down towards the clubs and asked a black man which club I should go to. He said either club was good and to thank him I offered him a fiver or a ten in payment, he took the ten. I then walked a little further down the street, smoking a cigar, and some younger guys offered me something that looked like crystal meth. I told them that no, I was good with my cigar and they angrily let me go. I continued down the street and went into another club, after paying the coverage. This one was amazing, the best yet. There was a girl hanging from the ceiling in a gold cage, and the girls on the poles were such amazing acrobats that I thought they had gotten power from the devil. A bunch of young guys were standing entranced by it all, while I calmly walked back to the private lap dance section and watched a private lap dance going down. The stripper giving the lap dance cast me a couple of coy glances and when she was done, came over and asked me, "Do you want a lap dance honey?" I declined because for some reason I had not brought enough money and then her voice became cold as ice. She coldly said this is a private dance area and you need to leave. I told her belligerently that I had paid my coverage and also that I was with the mafia, so I did not have to leave. I then moved over and bought a drink and watched the show for a bit longer.

While I was just chilling, a guy could not come up with the funds for a lap dance he had had and the stripper was getting nasty with him. I asked if I could help out and gave the stripper my last three dollars. She was so moved she gave me a big hug and said thank you. I told her I loved her and that is when she freaked out, I was talking about like the love of Christ, which I felt. But she totally thought I was sick in the head, and I guess she was right. I was wondering what was wrong with this crazy bitch and got a little support from a girl reading a book at a table nearby, who kind of shrugged and shook her head.

After leaving the club it was rather early in the morning and I was rolling to some Slim Shady, when a black lady on a curb asked me for a ride home. Being a kind hearted soul, at least in the state of mind I was in, I said sure. Pretty soon she was directing me to pick up some other black folks and we were heading to a late night bar. I bought her a drink and she bought me a drink and finally we were ready to head to her place with all the black folks she knew apparently. There was me and about five blacks and things were looking kind of scary for me. Finally we ended up at her place in Gresham and her and her sister and two black guys hop out of my car and invite me up to her apartment. I figured it was safest to just go with the flow, so I agreed. In the apartment things got down and dirty and very kinky after I found out that the two sisters were transsexual. They even had hermaphrodite porn playing on the television set. One of the black guys also went out and bought something he called acid mix and, I took some big hits out of a glass pipe; it did not really affect me much other than a sharp sensation in my lungs.

After an all-nighter the two ladies had to go to work, so I decided to take the two black guys to McDonald's and Starbucks in Vancouver. We rolled to McDonald's and then I dropped the guys off at respective destinations so they could do deliveries. I told them no deliveries from my vehicle because the Feds were already watching me.

I then spent the rest of the day at the Portland Art Museum because I figured that would be a good place for the Mafia to hang out. In my delusional state I thought that I was becoming popular in the Mafia and could be a target for a future leadership role. There are a few good restaurants next to the Portland Art Museum and I took advantage of a couple good meals, good conversation with some businessmen, and good wine. Not at these restaurants but at a few others I had a habit of impressing the waitresses by leaving a large silver coin or bar as a tip. This impressed them so much that they treated me like royalty. (Worth about thirty dollars at the time)

After I got back from the Portland Art Museum, I had overstayed my welcome at home and needed to find a new place to stay. I got ahold of my buddy Chase and he welcomed me up to Chehalis, Washington. I drove up to Chehalis and continued my clubbing lifestyle, along with relaxing, listening to music, and kicking back in the lawn chair and drinking beer, such as Hawaiian Longboard Lager, which was my favorite. Some of my favorite music was a soundtrack I had put together with Eminem, No Love (Eminem ft. Lil Wayne), Criminal (Britney Spears) and Pepper (Butthole Surfers). I also listened to a fair bit of Ice Cube. I also enjoyed longboarding to a corner store and one day I picked up a six pack of Miller High Life; another day I settled for Blue Moon.

Before I moved from Vancouver, I took a quick trip to Hooters to see what that was all about; kind of an anticlimax from the club scene, but the waitresses treated me right. One of the Hooters waitresses even sat down and chatted with me and offered me the Hooters Calendar. She told me that once she had lived with a bunch of guys and enjoyed walking around in her bra and underwear. She said they told her it was making them feel weird and she had to stop.

Across the street from Chase's place there lived a family with a couple of girls a bit younger than me and I enjoyed showing them my possessions such as my large air rifle, my SOG Special Forces knife and my Four Loco, which I dumped out on the ground, I didn't like the taste of it. I wanted the girls to think I was Special Forces and I had some top secret missions I would disappear on. In reality, I was looking for new clubs in Tacoma and later on, searching for a prostitute from Tijuana, Mexico. Some days I would spend the day shooting my air rifle at beer cans in the back yard and smoking cigarettes to calm my nerves and give me a steadier shot.

17 All Black Club

After I swung by the Tacoma Hooters, my final mission in this country was to find a strip club in Tacoma. In Tacoma, I had heard of the Hill Top Crips and I wanted to meet some of them and start relations for a consolidation of power later on. I drove up to the Hill Top and parked my car in a gravel lot where I saw three guys that looked like they could be Crips. I quickly ran in between some semi-truck trailers and waited as the three guys walked up with their right hands in their pockets as if they might have a gun. I took my pack of smokes from my pocket and slid it across the back of a semi-truck trailer to the nearest "Crip" he grabbed the pack which had three cigarettes in it, one for each. They all lit up smokes and threw the pack carelessly on the ground. A white Tahoe then pulled up and picked all three of them up, neatly orchestrated.

Later that night I was driving around looking for the strip club and asking around, nobody could tell me where one was. I finally ended up next to some neon lights by what looked like a club. I walked towards the club and next to a car by the curb. A girl was giving me the evil eye as if I did not belong there and I confronted her. After shouting at her another car with a bunch of black guys pulled up and things looked to start getting heated. Finally, she started to cry and got into the car. I then went to the club and the door man a, tall black guy, said I was ok to go in. Inside the club it was filled with only blacks. I imagined that this was the Crip paradise. There were some girls, but none that were completely white. There were some strobe lights which played some odd music that sounded like machine gun fire and in the corner there was a big black object which looked like a coffin with some guys all sitting around it. I grabbed a drink and then started to make friends and hand out a little cash. Some of the guys would talk to me and some would not. That club was quite an experience and I felt that not only was I probably the only white guy that had ever been in there, I probably was lucky to get out of there with my skin intact.

Another day at Chase's house I was bored in the evening and he suggested I shoot some pool at a local establishment called the Olympic. I drove to the Olympic and walked in. The place was dark and full of people. At the counter was one seat that looked like it could be open, it had an umbrella on it and was right next to a pretty girl. She invited me to sit down and it turned out she was a worker at the Olympic, but was likely off duty. She was busy counting her tip money which was quite a stack of bills. She commented that the night had been good and asked me if I would like anything to drink. I told her to order me up a Dirty Martini. When the drink arrived I tried it and hated the taste of it; it tasted salty and oily and I was not willing to finish it. She asked me if I would like to go with her to the other side of the bar, where it was quieter; I said I would like that, so we went to a quieter area where I ordered a Margarita. We talked about life and I told her I went to the Old Apostolic Lutheran Church, but had not been going as often because it was a bit of a drive from Olympia and I was also interested in trying new things. She invited me to her church, a Crossroads Church, the next day, which happened to be Sunday.

The next day she called me up and made sure I was coming and I met her in the entry way of the church. We sat down together and listened and watched the Sermon. Afterword she introduced me to her boyfriend, who played in the church band. I was disappointed to find out she had a boyfriend but she had to go to work later anyway. After church I went to a bible study group with some church folks where we discussed a spot in the bible. I gave my thought and then later on, after a cup of coffee, headed back to Chase's place.

18 Mexico

Back at Chase's I planned my next mission, to go to Mexico and find a prostitute. Chase and his dad, who was visiting, were all for the mission. However, they said if I ended up in jail they were not going to be able to bail me out. I took off for Mexico and stayed one night in a Motel Six. I then stopped in Los Angeles and took a side exit to explore the ghetto. Before I left for LA, I had sent Ice Cube a personal note using the help files on his website. I told him I would be his personal bodyguard for 150k a year. He probably never got the note and I never saw him in LA. However, I did park my car in a shady graffiti ridden section of town and seeing a local bar I walked in. There were a few guys chilling at the bar when I rolled in with my skateboard. They were very friendly and offered to buy me a beer and I also got a free bag of pretzels. I showed them my SOG knife and one of the guys pulled out his pig sticker, which looked like a screwdriver, and said that he would get less time for his weapon than I would for mine.

I then ended up in Tijuana, Mexico a little earlier than the reservations I had made and ended up driving to a cheap motel called the Mayan. After parking I bartered for a room and got one fairly cheap. I was kind of hungry, so I went out for a walk looking for food. It was dark and I was not in what looked like a good section of Tijuana, if there is a good section. I walked by a few rough looking characters, with all the confidence in the world, and then visited a convenience store where I bought a liter of Finlandia Vodka and headed back to my motel room. At the motel room I downed the entire bottle and did not feel a bit drunk. I then went to bed and woke up late in time to search out my first club.

The first club I went in wasn't really a strip club, but the ladies were basically all naked. The oldest lady who looked like the lead over the younger ladies quickly spotted me and had me buy her a drink. She was probably about 36 or 37 and still looking pretty good. I was dressed for success with nice clothes and a three hundred and fifty dollar watch. After we sat down, she was in my lap, she tounged me a little and then proceeded to show me pictures of her cat and her daughter. She then wanted me to take shots of my tequila and it was so strong I spit it on the floor. She laughed and we then discussed prices, it would be $160 for sex which was more then I wanted to spend. She then fondled me and said we could try something different, which would be cheaper. It ended up that I got a cut rate hand job. At the end she said that she loved me and I found a taxi driver to show me the way back to the motel. At the motel, he asked me if I wanted some cocaine and just going with the flow, I said sure. He sold me five lines for twenty dollars and poured them out for me. He then rolled up a dollar bill for me and I proceeded to sniff all five lines; amazingly enough, nothing happened to me except my heart beat a little faster than usual, maybe the cocaine was cut.

The next day I headed into downtown TJ to do a little exploring. However, after I had parked my car a man compelled me to come into another club with him. This club was not as good as others I had been to but since I was there I bought a beer and sat with an older fortyish lady. She kept trying to get me to buy more, but I was getting sick of spending money and told her no. She then started using threatening language, but another individual at the club, noticing that I did not want to spend money, must have thought I needed some. He came up to my table and asked me if I wanted to do a drive for him. Not sure what kind of drive he wanted me to do, but sensing an opportunity to make money, I said sure. He then, with little explanation, proceeded to direct me to a new motel, which he would pay for. I was a little disappointed, because I was missing out on the nice motel I had reservations for, but I no longer had much choice. He had taken my car to do some repairs to it and had left me at the motel. That afternoon I took a walk with what appeared to be a gay man, since he kept staring at me. I decided it would be best to just humor him, so we took a little walk to the beach. He didn't speak English, so not a word was spoken the entire time; however the beach was nice.

That evening I decided to complete my mission and find a prostitute. I called a taxi and told the driver I wanted to find a prostitute. He told me that there was an abundant selection of prostitutes on a strip called La Revolution. He took me down there and I told him he could pick one out for me. He picked a nice looking light skinned Mexican woman in her twenties and we headed up to a room. In the room she asked me if I wanted sucky sucky and since I thought that was demeaning to woman, I said no. I then told her I wanted her to be on top and twenty minutes and forty dollars later, that was that; it cost an extra twenty for her to take off her shirt. Then I paid five more to the man that kept watch outside and 45 dollars later I was on my way.

The next day my car pulled up with the repairs complete. I found out later that they had not only fixed my vacuum leak, they had also built a compartment to store a young Mexican woman whom I would be transporting across the border. I was driven in my car to near the border and I would continue on alone. I had a cellphone provided to me by the Coyotes, people smugglers, and I was supposed to figure out which lane to take at the border, because apparently someone at the border was bought off. I called in and figured out the correct lane but all to no avail. I was supposed to get 1500 dollars for a successful run, but unfortunately I was searched at the border and found out. When the border guard came to my window he asked if he could search the back and I said sure. He lifted up where the spare tire goes in the back of my car and said "fuck there's a body in the back!", he then held a gun to my head and told me to get out of the car.

19 PRISON

 I spent a few days in this holding cell with very low quality burritos to eat and no place to get any sleep. I then was loaded in to a transport and hauled to a prison in downtown San Diego. Everywhere I went from then on out I was shackled hand and foot, until I was released. If I traveled with a group of inmates we were shackled together by the legs.

At the prison in down town San Diego, I soon learned that the best floor and the one that everyone wants to get to is floor eleven, the medical floor. I spent my time on some other floors but eventually I dislocated my shoulder in a freak accident and was transported to the medical floor. My shoulder had already been dislocated in a mental hospital earlier, so I was doing nothing but trying to move my mattress and it popped out, the pain once again was terrible.

During my entire stay in prison and beyond, I was manic and delusional. Nobody in prison was giving me any medication, so I continued to live in a dream world surrounded by undercover government agents and the Mafia. The interesting part about it is that there very well could have been both undercover agents of the government and also mafia members in prison.

There was a definite chain of command in prison both official and unofficial. Certain people could get things done or get information about what events like transports would happen in the future. Before I had ended up in prison I had watched a lot of mafia movies to learn more about them and I ran into a young fellow that had a moustache in exactly the Sicilian style. One evening he was able to get me extra food in the food line. Another day he invited me to a cake feed in his cell. He had a bunch of large squares of cake, possibly left over from another meal but I'm not sure how he got his hands on them. At another time when I was getting ready to leave the medical floor to go to another prison an older man who seemed to be in charge, or able to get his way on the floor, organized a taco feed for me and took over the kitchen to make the tacos. I had ordered up a lot of the ingredients from commissary with money my parents had put on my account. Even when you received commissary the prisoners took care of distributing it and the people distributing took a small cut of everything. For example, if you were receiving four packs of Ramen noodles they might take one of them. It didn't pay to complain about the system because if you went along with it you could get ahead and soon be chilling with front row seats to the TV.

Speaking of front row seats to the TV, it took me two or three weeks of befriending the man in charge of our area before I was allowed a seat close to the TV. I would tell him stories of how powerful I was in the Portland Mafia and also rat out people to him that I thought were undercover government agents. Finally he allowed me to move closer to the table, but I still could not hear the TV because you would hear it through a certain channel on a radio, if you had one.

A typical day on the medical floor would be waking up around 7:30 A.M., making the bed in a navy style because the official head of our floor was former navy, eating breakfast, chilling out and watching TV along with reading and bs'ing, eating lunch, going play volleyball around 1:00, coming back with more chilling and bs'ing, eating dinner and going to bed. If you wanted you could do pull ups and dips on some bars next to a TV.

Finally after about three weeks I was informed by my buddy that let me sit closer to the TV that I was to be transported to another prison, he said he would write me. As a couple of side notes before I move on to the next prison. People had razors that they obtained by breaking shavers apart and taking out the razor blades and they also had sharpened plastic spoons and pencils. There was good reason to follow the hierarchy on the prison floor or you could get hurt bad. If you were just chill and didn't steal anybody's snickers bars, more on that later, everything was all good.

I was loaded up on a prison bus and transported to a private prison closer to the Mexican border. When I arrived there was intake where we had to be checked over by a nurse, or at least a nurse's helper. The nurse's helper checking me out was young and pretty and seemed to like me. She would check me over a few more times before I was done with California Correctional Facility.

When I arrived in general population, Gen Pop as they call it, every cell was very full and I was given a tub to sleep in and pointed to a cell with two white guys. Before too long though I had to have a meeting with who was in charge of the whites on the floor and told the rules. Take showers daily, and work out at yard. Once again everything was chill as long as you followed the rules. Otherwise, you would be beat down by many individuals. I remember thinking that no matter where you are you are subject to rules, even if there did not have to be any rules the inmates made them up.

On the floor were three groups of individuals, in three different groups. Mexicans born in the USA, Mexicans born in Mexico, and the whites, if there were any blacks they were also in their own group. Another rule that was not as strictly enforced but was in existence was no sharing the black man's food.

In the first pod I was in I would spend my days talking to people and learning their life stories. Everyone was happy to talk about their experiences and many of the experiences were very different from the way I had grown up going to the Old Apostolic Lutheran Church. One black guy who I spent a lot of time with talked about how he had made millions growing pot and he alluded to the fact that he still had a lot of money on the outside. My cell mates, the white guys, had got busted for people smuggling but from the sounds of it, they had been in and out of jail for years. One of them even said he had been on America's most wanted for a while. Both of my cell mates seemed like the devils servants, talking about large Meth infused parties where one of them thought it was funny to get people that were against Meth, like a drug therapist, hooked on Meth.

While in that first pod, I would make trips to the church service they had on Sunday and check out books that I thought looked interesting. While in prison I read the Book of Masons, as well as the Koran. Both books were interesting but I still prefer the bible.

When I was not reading, watching TV, or visiting with people I would play ping pong with a younger guy who was locked up too. One time we bet for some Ramen noodles and my cell mates even threw in a little commissary. I just barely lost and we were all disappointed.

Another important daily event was yard. We worked out at yard, which was a large concrete pad surrounded by razor wire. The pad had a basketball hoop and also a pull up bar. I would shoot hoops, do burpees, and pullups. Burpees were not as important at the first pod I was in but at a later pod they were critical. The second pod I went to was run by a Nazi Skinhead, and he loved to do three hundred burpees at a time. I would do around a hundred.

After about a month in the first pod I asked to be switched to another pod where I hoped there would be more room and maybe my own bunk in a cell. I was switched to another pod and placed with a couple of individuals who stank like dead bodies. I complained bitterly and was switched again to another cell. This cell was a little better as I was sharing it with a Mexican who worked in the kitchen. One day he brought me a large peanut butter sandwich, which was excellent. This was only a temporary switch though and I was then moved in with a white guy who I swore was gay.

One day I caught him giving another man a back massage on my bed. Another day he was lifting up my blanket and staring at my back. He did however have a lot of commissary as he claimed he was a retired Auditor and he was willing to share a little food each night as well as some of his coffee. In my delusional state of mind though I was not happy with how much he was giving me as he had a huge stack of commissary. When he was gone, I consulted with God and determined that it would be okay if I took some of his snickers bars. Over a few days' time I took five of them and they were excellent. Then he noticed they were gone and asked if anyone had been in our cell. I told him that no, no one had been in our cell and that I had taken them. He became very angry and began pounding the wall with his fist. He then told me that I was going to have to leave the cell. I left the cell but soon he was not happy with that and told the guard that I was going to have to leave the pod. The guard asked me what happened and I told him and was then sent to solitary.

Before I was sent to solitary a little more about the NAZI Skinhead that was running the pod I was kicked out of and about interesting pod activities. He had a large tattoo that said peckerwood on his stomach and a large red swastika tattooed on his chest and neck. He would run the pod floor with an iron fist and threaten to go sharpen spoons or pencils if anyone got out of line. He also had the largest collection of books, since he was in charge. I would stay on his good side by doing burpees with him at yard. There was another chill smaller guy in the same pod with the NAZI Skinhead. He was in for people smuggling but he had been in and out of jail and prison his entire life. He was an exceptional artist and would make artwork, like roses, to draw on envelopes that inmates would then use to send letters to their girlfriends. He would receive commissary from the other inmates for doing the artwork. Another interesting note was that one of our jail guards was a professional bantam weight boxer; we saw one of his fights on the TV one day, he was very nice. Finally, individuals in the pods liked to figure out how to make moonshine and the artist liked to save up his peaches and try to get yours, along with candy and other ingredients and then put this all in a bottle and let it sit for a while and ferment. If you were caught making hooch in prison you could get a charge for manufacturing but no one seemed to care. Just as the inmates were willing to beat you down for an infraction of their own rules, at the risk of lengthening their own prison sentence, they were willing to take the risk of manufacturing alcohol for a longer prison sentence if caught. In reality, charges did not seem to be brought against inmates very often.

Just because you are in solitary does not mean you are in a cell alone. I shared many cells in solitary, but because of my erratic behavior I was not able to keep a cell mate for too long. The pattern was usually that they shared their entire life story with me and then things began to get uncomfortable so somebody had to leave. Each day in solitary we got to go out to an outside cell to experience the fresh air and while I was outside one day I ran into another guy I had been with in general population. He teased me about the snickers stealing escapade and said that everyone was now calling me snickers. Out at the solitary yard I kept up my routine of Burpees and on the low calorie diet with the exercise I lost fifty pounds and came out pretty thin and ripped. At some point the prison warden had a meeting and tried to return me to general population, which did not work. When I tried to return to the pods the leaders of the whites in each pod told me that I would have to leave or "it would be all bad." They told me that it was rumored that I could not follow the rules, so I would have to go back to solitary.

I'll tell a little story about one of my cell mates, in solitary, who I will call The Captain, since he told me that that is what his friends used to call him. It sounded like he was really something in his day but his flame burned out, probably due to Meth, and he is now Schizophrenic and on Disability and Social Security. He was caught transporting Meth across the border; from the sounds of it he was doing a job for his brother who was pretty high up in the Mexican Mafia. Some of the time we would discuss religion and at other times he would brag about how he had had sex with numerous virgins when he was younger and enjoyed making them bleed. After we had been together for a week or two he told me he would get his brother to put fifty dollars on my commissary account, a gesture that I greatly appreciated.

When I got the fifty I ordered up a good stock of grub along with a radio to help while the time away. The radio proved to be a Godsend because once I got that the time went by much faster. I would spend my time listening to music and singing along. I also had feelings of grandiosity, so I thought that the artists were creating new music just for me. Eventually my batteries would run out but I convinced the Prison Staff that I needed more for my mental health. I think they gave in because it truly kept me from raising a ruckus if I had a radio that worked. On a side note, I noticed that you could get a little more life out of your batteries if you soaked them in hot water, or so I was told and so it seemed.

Finally, it was time to leave the Captain because we got in a fight. The Captain had some pictures he had gotten from relatives and I thought they were my pictures. Especially one of a cute girl named Brooklyn. I had stolen the picture of Brooklyn and he told me to give him the picture back. I told him that I would not do that and angry with him I slapped him on the back. He then proceeded to grab me by the nuts, probably something learned from his dad a marine, and I grabbed him by the throat. I then shit my pants and told him I had to leave. I called the guard on the PA system and told him I had to leave.

There were three or four other people I was with in solitary but eventually I could not get along with anyone and I was in a cell by myself. Some time I would get bored because my batteries would run out on my radio, and/or I could not see the TV. One day I decided it was time to make a trip to a medical cell where I knew I would be able to see the TV. I began to holler and scream and throw water all over my cell. The guards came over and asked me what I wanted and I told them I wanted to go to medical. They then came over a little while later to transport me and I had changed my mind. I no longer wanted to go. They then decided I was going anyway and brought in an extraction team. An extraction team was made up of what looked like eight or so riot police all dressed in black with shields and face shields. They then opened the flapper where the food goes in on your cell and threw in a canister of mace. The mace got in my eyes and I was choking feeling like I was going to suffocate. They then opened the door to get me to leave and I cooperated exactly as they wanted me to, so I did not get hurt. They transported me to a room with padded walls and I did constant pushups until the pain went away. I was then later transported to medical where I could watch the TV, woo hoo.

After getting back from medical I spent some time with a few more cell mates and heard there life's stories. One of them had a love affair with Pot and had gotten caught trying to transport a truckload of it across the border. Another got caught with weed in a motor home he was in.

Every once in a while I would meet with my public defender but in the state I was in I was not really able to assist him or even competent to stand trial. He did have a psychiatrist come in and evaluate me, but I am not really sure what the decision was because my attorney decided that I did not appear crazy enough to convince a jury of an insanity plea. This is unfortunate as I already had a Not Guilty By Reason of Insanity on my record from another incident and with a decent attorney it probably would not have been difficult to convince a jury that I was suffering another breakdown.

After eight months in prison I was given a plea deal to get time served in addition to three years of probation. At about ten o'clock at night I was released from San Diego Correctional Facility with no warning phone call to my parents and really no forewarning to anybody. My mom had specifically talked to the prison and they had told her that they would let her know when I would be released, so they could arrange transportation for me. Instead the prison loaded a few of us up in a van and we headed for downtown San Diego. About ten thirty at night they opened the door of the transport and we got out. I had nothing but .80 cents to my name and a passport. I was supposed to check in with the Department of Corrections for probation within a day but in my current state of mind I did not pay any attention to that and threw my probation paperwork off a bridge.

20 HUNGRY

They had taken everything I had at the Mexican border, which included a $350 Bulova watch, a SOG knife and my wallet with my ID and credit cards, also my car. I thought that they had kept my personal effects, so I decided that the first thing I would do was to walk to the border and get them. It would be around a twenty mile walk in Croks, with no food, but I did not know that so I decided to follow the rail line and start walking. After a while I found some bushes and went to sleep for a bit. I then continued walking and after quite a few miles was given a short ride to the next town. The man also gave me a dollar and I went into the gas station and bought a fun size snickers bar. I then continued walking all the while thinking that I was being watched and possibly helped out a little by the Roman Catholic Church. I thought the Roman Catholic Church was part of a New World Order type of power system. In the morning I was still walking and a police gave me a short ride. On the walk I found a cell phone and when I got to the border I was able to trade it for six cigarettes. At the border I asked about my stuff and they told me they had sent me notices to prison asking me if I wanted them to keep my stuff and since I had not replied they assumed I was not coming back and they destroyed everything but my car. The car I could not have back unless I was to pay for storage costs which were more than the car was worth.

So ravenously hungry I turned for the walk back to San Diego where I would call my parents collect and take the Grey Hound home. The time I was released from prison was in February and it was fairly cold and somewhat rainy. I was getting damp and chilled to the bone as I trudged along and I swung into a gas station where I was told I could have some free coffee, I loaded the coffee with creamer so I would have more energy. I then spent a few more nights under the weather before a police officer transported me over the river from Coronado, California to San Diego, since I could not cross that bridge on foot.

One of the nights under the weather I covered myself with sand and the other night I found what looked like a bums nest and camped out there. The nest even had a damp coat for me to wear. Just before I covered myself with sand, late at night, I ended up at a military base by accident. An army guard told me I was in a private area and I told him I was sorry I did not know. I then, being very hungry, asked him if he had any food, he had a little bit of some leftover food and I ate that, it was just what I needed.

Back in San Diego I got ahold of my parents and they bought me a Grey Hound ticket home. While I waited for the Grey Hound a black man sidled over to me and asked me if I wanted a drink of some blue liquid he had in a Gatorade bottle. I said sure, and after taking a pull or two my belly felt nice and warm. It was some good drink, and I was not hungry for a while.

I got on the Greyhound and the first stop was Weed California. I hopped out and wished I had one of the six cigarettes I smoked earlier to celebrate being in Weed California where I imagined all of the weed was grown. We then continued on our way and made another stop at a Burger King, but since I had no money I was forced to go hungry. I finally did get a plate of nachos after a black guy showed mercy on me and gave me five dollars. He also gave me another dollar after he saw I bought food with the first five he gave me.

Finally I arrived in Portland, probably about thirty hours later, and after getting off the bus I had a raging headache. I walked into the bathroom and tried to get rid of it by pounding my head against a bathroom stall. Nobody was there to pick me up because, I learned later, I had overstayed on at least one stop and that put me behind schedule.

I decided to just take off walking because I got kicked out of the Greyhound terminal because of pounding my head against the bathroom stall; in fact the security lady threatened to tase me if I did not leave, so I left. On the way to my next destination, a grocery store, I bummed another cigarette. In the store I must have looked a site, with a large beard and the coat I found in the bums nest. I noticed that this grocery store had free wine samples, so I had a small cup of wine. I then proceeded to call my mom and dad up and shortly thereafter they picked me up.

21 HOME

Back at home it was nice to see everyone but because I was now a lot trimmer after prison there was something I needed to do. I found my pin-stripe suit, the one I had won a business plan competition at Gonzaga University with and put it on; it fit perfect. Next up I had to find a package of my Al Capone Cognate Dipped miniatures and have a few. The problem was that I could not find the Al Capone's, so I decided to settle for a Black and Mild another type of cigar, not as classy.

The next Sunday I still had my beard and I decided to go to church, as I always do on Sundays. Perhaps people though I looked strange but they never said anything. After church, or maybe the next day, I shaved off my beard and left nothing but a small mustache which looked to me like the Sicilians had seen in the Mafia movies. I thought that everything I was doing was being watched by cameras; so many times I decided to put on a show for the cameras. My brother still complains bitterly about how I ruined his good razor shaving off a big beard and then left most of the hair in the sink.

The next day I decided to go to the unemployment office to get my paperwork squared away so I could start getting cash flow again. The problem was, I thought that satellites were watching me and that it would be cool to open up the door on a newer mustang to see if it was locked, turns out the Mustang was open but somebody called me in and I was transported to jail because I had an outstanding warrant. The warrant was outstanding from a missed hearing for supervised release. I was on supervised release because I had gotten a Not Guilty By Reason of Insanity earlier for driving 120 MPH, or so, on my Ninja Super-sport 650; more on that story in another chapter.

The cops, who I thought were federal agents, approached me very carefully and searched me. I had a Zippo lighter which I liked to pretend was modified to shoot twenty two bullets and they checked that over carefully. I was then transported to the Clark County Jail and then after a few days transported to Pearce County Jail. On the way up to Pearce County they transported me in a little box and I remember thinking that government agents were testing me to see how I could handle small confined spaces. After I reached Pierce County Jail they left me there for about a week and a half to await my hearing. At my hearing my parents tried to tell the judge that I was out of my mind but my attorney cut them off and said that I had just been trying the handle on the newer Mustang to see if the car alarm worked. I was then released but my driving privileges were taken away for a few weeks.

During those weeks I drove my bike around everywhere or I walked. One day I drove about sixteen miles round trip to a smoke shop in Brush Prairie, Washington smoking the entire way there and back. I also listened to my personal soundtrack which included Eminem.

After a while I started to scream in the house and get angry about something and my mom called the police. They once again hauled me to Clark County Jail and I once again had a warrant outstanding in Pierce County for my supervised release because I had failed to make a hearing. I was brought up to Pierce County where I was quickly placed in solitary because I started screaming and acting out. I spent a few months in solitary while the Feds tried to take me back to San Diego because I had missed a probation appointment. My attorney tried to get me sent to Western State Hospital, so I could get stabilized, but the feds were not listening. Finally, after a few months of me getting crazier and crazier in solitary my parents were told by a family friend to contact US Rep Jamie Herrera Beutler and after they wrote a letter to her I was transported. By getting crazier and crazier in solitary, I mean that I would start screaming and cursing everyone that tried to come talk to me and at one point I ripped off my shirt and tore it apart with my bare hands. On another occasion I would spin around the cell playing with toilet paper.

22 WESTERN STATE

Finally I was cuffed and loaded up into a police car and driven to Western State Hospital. This would be my second time at the hospital. At an earlier time I had spent three months at Western State Hospital getting stabilized so that I would be competent to stand trial. When I arrived at the hospital I was checked over by a pretty nurse with red hair and then I was questioned by a panel of officials. At the time I had extreme delusions of grandeur, so I'm sure my answers were very arrogant. Finally, I was released into the main room with the rest of the patients.

The ward that I was on was for individuals that had committed crimes but had been proven to have some kind of mental condition that made them eligible to be a patient at Western State instead of going to prison. Many were there for murder, others for assault, and others for rape. Most of the patients preferred to be at Western State because they were labeled as patients instead of as inmates. There also was a friendlier atmosphere at Western State than at prison. The floor was not so much controlled by groups of inmates like in prison.

When I got onto the main floor I begin to make a lot of noise, jump over furniture, and flash gang signs. The hospital staff told me to sit down in a chair and they stabbed a needle in me that was supposed to calm me down; it did not work. During the first few days at Western State I was acting a little crazy, but after a few weeks of medication; a large dose of Risperidone and Lithium, I stabilized and for the remainder of the nine months I was a model patient. Some of the patients even remarked, when I was being released, about how surprising it was that a patient like me was being released after only nine months; many of them had been there for years.

After the first two or three weeks I stabilized and then reality hit me. I had three years left of my supervised release and I could be left in Western State for the entire time. I panicked making a call to my attorney and questioned him on if there was a way I could get out soon. He said that I might just have to wait it out until the Risk Review board met, which was a board that meets periodically to discuss patients cases and if their condition has improved enough so that they would be an asset to the public. In their meetings the risk review board would also discuss patient's levels and whether a patient's level should be moved up or taken down.

From the other patients and by talking to staff I learned that the Risk Review Board likes to see an individual at the highest level, a level seven, before they even consider releasing them to the public. I started out as a level one with much room for improvement. Since the board met once a month I would be at Western State for a minimum of seven months, because they would only move one level a month at the most.

While amazingly enough I became quite stable very quickly, once they had adjusted my medication up high enough, the Risk Review

Board wanted to see a track record of good behavior, which included going to classes every day, getting out of bed, listening to staff, taking advantage of work opportunities like working in the store, etc. Years earlier I had been diagnosed with bipolar one disorder and after many years was still in the process of finding the proper dosage of medication. Too high of a dosage would lead me to be incapable of functioning as normal in society, but too low of a dosage would cause me to go manic, psychotic and/or delusional. I had been on this cycle of doing fine followed by a breakdown ever since 2007 and now was 2012. With at least seven months remaining at Western State but a maximum of three years, I felt panicky and like I wanted to beat my head against the wall. I asked for an Adavan to calm me down and I found out later that that got logged into my medical history as a negative occurrence. After a while I finally calmed down and started going through the daily routine and getting to know the people with me.

Every day we got up at seven thirty and ate a light breakfast. We then went to classes until noon. Classes covered topics such as mental illnesses, famous actors with mental illness, art classes, and another class where we just watched movies. One important thing that we worked on in a class was a Wellness, Recovery, Action, Plan, (WRAP), which covered topics such as what types of healthy activities you could take part in to cope with your illness, what type of support network you would have when you got out, and so on. This plan was important because the risk review board was interested in seeing it as concrete proof that you were ready to get out of the hospital.

We went out to yard twice a day and I would visit with friends I had made and would also jog a majority of the time. We were out for about half an hour at a time and I would jog around three miles. A young guy named Jim would often jog with me and would talk to me about crazy business ideas he planned to do once he got out of Western State; the problem was, he could never remain stable on medications for long and would move up a few levels and then have a breakdown and move back down to the lowest levels; he probably had Schizophrenia. One day when he had a breakdown he started kicking the Plexiglas windows around the nurse's station and screaming; another time he tried to fight someone. Fortunately, while I was at Western State no one got too violent, at least on my unit, on another unit someone was killed with a sharpened pencil. At different times the staff would take away all of the pencils and pens from the wards and only allow small flexible pens.

Life went on at Western State month after month. Each breakfast, go to yard, go to classes, have a morning meeting where we discussed mental health issues, talk to a nurse about how we were doing, have a random inspection of the rooms, plan for a party on special occasions and so on. On the weekends we would watch TV, go to the gym if we were a level three and above, get visitors, and go to church. On all the slack time, we could read, watch TV, check out the TV and bring it to our room for a movie, and eat popcorn and visit. The weekends were always long because there were no classes, but we would make popcorn and go to the gym and play basketball. If we were the right level we could also workout in a small weight room. I jumped through the levels at about the rate of one level a month and was soon able to go to the gym and the weight room.

With every level came increased privileges and months later I would be working in a store and helping clean up class rooms for pay. With an increase in your levels you could also begin to see visitors. My parents, friends, and our church pastors would make the two hour drive up to visit me and I really enjoyed those visits. Often my parents and friends would bring up some food for me to eat which was also an excellent change of diet. Being locked up, it was really something to see your friends and talk about Christianity, or what was going on outside of Western State.

About nine months later, in December of 2012 I finally was Okayed to leave by the Western State Risk Review Board. My attorney finalized the paper work and it was faxed over from the judge and just before Christmas I was released. I was elated and my mom and dad almost did not believe it was true. I had finally reached a level seven and had the ability to walk around Western state with a key card. (I would often walk to the visitor's room alone and buy a cinnamon roll along with a bottle of pop, from the money I had made working, which was a big treat.) I also had been working in the Western State Hospital Store, as well as helping out clean classrooms for pay. The risk review board had determined that I would be a greater asset to the community as a free citizen then as a member confined at Western State Hospital. However, just because I was released from WSH did not mean I was completely free. I still had a few years of supervised release left and three years of probation left until I was truly free from the shackles of the law.

While at Western State I had filled out paperwork for Disability and Social Security, which was a shoo in because I had spent nine months in a mental hospital, along with three months in my earlier stay. On Disability it would have been a picnic other then I now had a criminal record which included a felony. In addition, I had two years of Clark County probation due to the trespassing incident, three years of federal probation due to the Alien Smuggling incident, and I also had a few more years of supervised release from my Not Guilty by Reason of Insanity, which was administered by the state. Having to juggle all of these obligations was challenging and anytime I wanted to go anywhere it was a real trial. I got to know my new probation officers who included a Federal gal by the name of Angie, a county officer by the name of Dave, and a state officer that kept changing.

23 AFTER THE BREAKDOWNS

Not content with doing nothing on Disability I decided to give another go at IT classes at Clark College. I took a few classes, one at a time, and pulled A's in them. I also started a part time job bookkeeping with a family friend and did that for about a year and a half until I ran out of work and decided I would rather spend time windsurfing and taking kiteboarding lessons. I had received a settlement for about seven thousand dollars from Social security, for all of the time I was not able to work because of my mental illness and I was also able to save around seven thousand dollars bookkeeping. In short, I had no money problems, but because of my probation I was not able to fully enjoy my money with some good travel.

I spent about a year working for Silvertrek systems bookkeeping while I was on probation and on the weekends in the summer I would go Windsurfing. A few years back I had bought a cheap windsurfing setup and after much hard work I was able to learn how to sail across the Columbia River and back. Windsurfing is relaxing and a lot of fun, when you get the hang of it but to learn it is a challenge. After windsurfing for a few summers I decided to try kiteboarding. Windsurfing there is a large sail and a board and kiteboarding there is a large kite and a smaller board. While windsurfers tend to be a little older kite boarding tends to be more popular among the younger generation. With kiteboarding you can catch massive amounts of air and it tends to be a little more extreme than windsurfing.

Bookkeeping at Silvertrek had been enjoyable but I was running out of work to do and I kept dreaming about getting more into Kiteboarding or Windsurfing for a summer. I ended up quitting a Silvertrek and I signed up for Kiteboarding lessons in the Columbia River Gorge. The lessons were expensive but it was a lot of fun and kind of stressful to learn how to Kiteboard. In a few days' time taking a few hours of lessons a day I learned how to control the large kite and was ready to learn how to include a board. Then I decided that it was just too stressful and expensive to get into kiteboarding and I decided to focus on windsurfing instead. With windsurfing you are not controlling a large expensive kite in the air which can get caught on a bridge, hit another kite boarder or drag you off your feet with a sudden gust of wind. Anytime you feel like the wind is too strong with a windsurf board you can just let go of the sail and let it hit the water. Also the windsurfing community is very tight knit and everybody is very supportive of one another. The older generation is very happy to see a young guy learning how to windsurf board and they will help you out with tips, tricks, and sometime even free gear. All in all, I decided that windsurfing is the better fit more me as it is more relaxing. While I have not been able to go windsurfing as much recently because I need some new gear I hope to do it again sometime as my finances improve.

Three years after getting out of Western State I had finished all of my probation obligations and was ready to take a trip to Europe, which I had waited on for quite a few years. I have many friends in Europe, specifically Scandinavia, and have travelled there numerous times.

Being on probation is a drag. After I got out of prison part of my plea deal was three years of Federal Probation. In addition to Federal Probation I also had State Supervised Release for when I was going too fast on my motorcycle and I had two years of County Probation for the trespassing incident. Unfortunately, the Federal, State, or the County did not work together, so each had a separate set of requirements and made contact with me in different ways and at different times.

The federal probation was the best to work with as they only swung by about once every three months and when they did they had no visible guns. The state probation swung by less often but the probation officers carried guns and were not as friendly. The county probation officer did not come by the house at all, but I had to swing by the office in downtown Vancouver about once a month.

Having someone swing by your house at any time and check on you leaves you feeling under the gun and somewhat stressed out all the time. In addition, to them swinging by I would have to fill out trip permits and ask permission every time before I planned a trip. Even if I was going only a few hours away to Seattle, which I did one time to visit friends and go to church meetings, I would need to get permission from at least the County Probation. With the federal probation I had permission to travel from the Canadian border to Portland, Oregon, and I could travel anywhere with the state probation, but with the county probation I was not allowed to travel outside of Clark County.

In addition to having to ask permission before travel I would be called in to the Federal Office at random times to take a pee test. Also, when I was working at an office doing bookkeeping, my federal probation officer, a younger woman, would always threaten that she was going to visit my workplace and talk with my employers. Thinking about her coming in to the office put additional stress on me because even though my co-workers were friends from church, we also shared the office space with others who might not understand why I was on probation.

On a few different days when I was taking naps in the afternoon one of my probation officers would knock on my door and ask me to open up because they wanted to talk to me. I would open the door in my pajama pants and invite either Erika my Federal PO in or my State PO's in to visit. Erika was a shorter dark haired lady around forty and actually quite pretty. My state PO's were fat and ugly and carried forty fives, they also had large DOC labels across their chests. The state PO's kind of made my mom and dad nervous because of their appearance and the large guns, also their attitudes were not as friendly. Erica was friendly, but professional. She wore a light blue jacket and likely had a bullet proof vest underneath, whether she had a gun or not, I never found out.

After three years I got off of all of my probation and I was ready for my trip to Europe I had planned. Probation was tough and it really taught me the value of freedom. After I got back from Europe I sent Erika an e-mail letting her know that I had had no trouble with travel to Europe and I was able to invite her to church. She replied with a thank you and said that it really seemed that my travels to Europe had done me good.

I took off for Europe on the twelfth of November and planned to come back on the twentieth of January. I planned to spend a good part of my time in Finland, but also some time in Norway, Sweden and a few other European countries. Europe was fantastic; I had no trouble with travel even though I was now a Convicted Felon. Other than Finland, Sweden, and Norway, I chose to travel to Greece and France; four days in Athens and three days in Paris.

In Greece I stayed at a hostel and spent a few days traveling with a Mexican girl I met on a tour. It was epic with a late night coffee on a high-rise overlooking Athens and excellent meals and company. She was a medical student who lived in Guadalajara. I then traveled to Paris and hung out with a guy from my church that lived there, at least in the evenings. I saw the Eiffel Tower, the Louvre Museum and other famous sights. Finally, I flew back to Finland and spent some time going to church meetings. Back home I started looking for work with the long-term goal of getting off of Disability and Social Security. Finding suitable employment can be a real challenge with a Felony and two Misdemeanors. Also, I am somewhat limited by how much stress I can take on, as my brain does not function at quite one hundred percent. After a few months of working with an employment specialist I was able to find a part time job working for a company called Appraisals Plus. Also, I started volunteering on Fridays at NAMI, National Alliance for the Mentally Ill. Finally, NAMI helped me fill out a Presidential Pardon petition and that is still in line to be decided upon.

You may ask what gave my mom and dad the ability to welcome me back to the fold after each breakdown. I believe the deciding factor in accepting me back each time was my mom and dad's faith in the doctors, the medication, and their faith in God. When a person is properly medicated and of a sound mind you can tell they will be fine in a number of ways, you can hear their stability in conversation, what actions they are taking to better their lives and you listen to the doctor's opinion, which may not be always right. Sometimes the clues to stability are subtle and can take longer to pick out. When you and the doctors are confident that a person is stable, it is easier to take them back home because you can be confident that the bout of illness is over and has been properly addressed.

After my diagnosis many of my brothers and sisters were diagnosed with Bi-Polar. One of them who we will call Joe suffered with violent thoughts which led him to see a psychiatrist and he began to take Lithium. For example, at work he would dream of killing the people he was working with and these troubling thoughts led him to see that he had a problem. Personally I have never had violent thoughts, but I did have strange thoughts that led me to question whether my brothers and sisters were evil and whether I would be doing the world a service if I killed them. I remember having one thought in particular that my brothers and sisters were no different than robins and that getting rid of them would not be a big deal.

Another brother did not have violent thoughts but he would just act zany, rapping Eminem and the like. He would also moon security cameras in the mental hospital. When I was manic I would act like a gangster, flashing gang signs and I also mooned a security camera at a mental hospital. This brother has also suffered from depression and sleeplessness which I have also suffered from but not to the extent that he has. Fortunately, my illness has been very treatable which cannot be said for some of my other siblings. A brother and sister of mine have had a lot of trouble finding a medication or combination of medications that will work for them.

When I am out of my mind but also when I am in my right mind I have a strong belief that my life is guided by a divine hand. Because I believe my life is so guided, when something goes wrong, like I end up in Jail, I take things in stride and believe that God has a plan even in this. While insane, getting in trouble with the law has very little impact on me. I don't feel feelings of regret or remorse for anything. When I get back to my right mind I have to believe, as part of my faith, that everything was part of God's plan and he will continue to guide my life. That does not mean that I have not felt depressed when faced with three years of Federal Probation, many years of Supervised Release, and two years of County Probation. Now that is all over, but having the law hanging over my head was definitely a depressant.

As you have read, throughout my illness I ended up being sentenced for various crimes and spending time in Jail, Prison, and on probation. Showing up for court while insane was just another day, and I was in no way capable of helping ensure a good outcome for myself. For example, when I went to court for the firearms charge and where I received the restraining order against my mother, I was lost in a dream world thinking that my name was Nathan Virtanen and that my mother and father wanted to kill me. In fact, when the judge asked my name I said that it was Nathan Virtanen.

By my second court hearing when I was stabilized I was so sick of being locked up in solitary confinement that I would have been happy anywhere, including on the street. The fact that I could not go home because of a restraining order did not matter to me in the least. I was just thankful I was being released at all. The fact that I ended up going to my grandma and grandpas made me happy, probably just as happy as if I was going home. I have always had a good relationship with Bob and Ruth as we grew up going to sauna, a Finnish steam bath, there every Saturday night. This relationship only became stronger with the trials that I went through; I have the hope of someday meeting them again in heaven where we can be together forever.

Now that Bob and Ruth are gone my relationship with them is over but I still have a large support network of family and friends. In fact I am the oldest of fourteen children and Bob and Ruth had thirteen children which means that I have many aunts and uncles and cousins. Having a large support network is helpful because you always have someone to visit with and share opinions. However, my immediate family at home, mostly my mom and dad are the most important. They can tell how I am doing as they have been through it all. My mom or dad would be the first to notice and tell me if I was slipping back into mania or depression. My brothers and sisters are more important to me to just hang out with and visit with when I can. I know that they too would and they have stepped in to help me when I needed a ride from or to a mental hospital, or need some other kind of support.

Everyone at church feels almost like family and my relationship with friends from church has only strengthened with time. It is amazing how many people know me and have told my parents that I have helped their son or daughter cope with a mental illness. Just knowing that what I have been through and seeing that I am still in the faith has been a big help to many.

Personally I tend to be a more self-sufficient person that thrives in almost any environment. Wherever I'm at be it a mental hospital, Prison, another country etc. I will make friends and survive and thrive. The ability to make friends wherever has been important to me because I often have been locked up far away from family and friends. Another facet of making friends and being away from family is a person's ability to be happy with this kind of situation. I tend to be just about as happy if I am away from family as with them, after all I have God with me wherever I go and I trust in that.

Finally, as I alluded to earlier, after a person has been locked up for a period of time everything on the outside has more meaning then it would otherwise. For example, when I was at Western State I remember walking around the walking track with a friend, who had killed his dad and had schizophrenia, and talking about how nice it would be to just go to the corner store and buy a Snickers bar or a bottle of pop. I got so sick of the healthy low calorie meals at Western State and prison that it was like heaven when I got out and was able to have a good meal. Even today I can be quite happy with much less because I have come from such bleak circumstances.

ABOUT THE AUTHOR

I HOPE YOU HAVE ENJOYED READING ABOUT
MY LIFE. TODAY, I WORK PART-TIME AS A REAL
ESTATE APPRAISER AND A BOOKKEEPER. I
LOVE TO TRAVEL AND HAVE A TRIP PLANNED
TO SCANDINAVIA SOON.

VICTOR WIRTANEN

Made in the USA
Lexington, KY
17 February 2018